CAN DO ANYTHING!

- the Miracle stories of "Banjo" Bill Leslie

by W. Paul Leslie

Foreword - Major Sam Fame®

The story of 'Banjo Bill' is the story of the grace of God at work! Bill's son, Paul Leslie, has highlighted many pieces of the Leslie puzzle to provide a brief but all-encompassing glimpse of 'an instrument' in the hands of God. In many ways I have journeyed with this man who had a huge impact and major influence on my life. How can I best describe him? He was a lover of God and a lover of souls. He was man with a heart of compassion, vision, fervent prayer and unbounding energy, and, in retrospect, a man with human frailties.

I remember the first time I met Bill Leslie. He was conducting a weekend spiritual campaign with 'his boys', the instrument- playing men often referred to as a 'combo', men from The Salvation Army's Harbour Light drug/alcohol rehabilitation program. It was 1962. I was active in The Salvation Army Kelowna Corps (church) in British Columbia, just 19, and a year away from entering The Salvation Army Officer

Training College in Toronto. Entering into a back room I couldn't help but overhear Bill passionately praying, prior to his conducting that evening's service. I can still hear the vibrant earnestness in his voice: "This poor man cried, and the Lord heard him, and saved him out of all his troubles". It wasn't until later that I understood Bill was 'praying scripture' (Psalm 34:6 KJV).

Over many years God continued to answer Bill's prayer for the thousands of men trapped on 'Skid Row', through the ministry

of Bill and his wife, Mildred, at Vancouver Harbour Light and Miracle Valley. Hosts of individuals were saved, transformed, delivered
and abundantly used of God in various ministries as 'Trophies of Grace'.

Once again, "This man cried"! This time it was for a physically sick and emotionally broken Bill Leslie. It was the excruciating cry of a burned-out man of God. Just think for a moment . . . 19 years of non-stop action:

opening and developing the First Harbour Light in Canada, unending expansion projects, weekly radio broadcasts, the development of Miracle Valley to provide long-term residential care, the Kispiox Miracle Valley Ranch Project in Northern British

Columbia to reach and minister to the First Nations Community, weekend campaigns preaching the Gospel near and far, while
encouraging 'his boys' to testify to God's saving grace. There was a never-ending round of speaking engagements and the establishment of other Harbour Light Centres in Western Canada. On and on it went... that constant, driving force... that one more soul might be saved, that one person more might be encouraged in their faith, that one more person or group might be moved to help with much needed finances. It was 19 years of non-stop, passionate ministry – no doubt at the expense of his own health and his relationship with his wife and the children he loved.

Brigadier Hilda Hansen, who worked so closely with Bill for many of the most challenging years, lovingly described him as a "man of God with feet of clay."

Bill had a total breakdown . . . a total 'burn-out'. Someone once said, "Burn-out happens when you have a fire burning in your soul!" Major Banjo Bill certainly had this 'burning fire in his soul'! I remember attending a Salvation Army Officer's Retreat when a fellow Officer was sharing a late night devotional. He was speaking of 'the one lost sheep'. The speaker then raised the astonishing question, "What happens when "the shepherd falls off the cliff?" Our thoughts are not so kind or forgiving when 'the shepherd' is himself the 'lost, hurting sheep'. Bill Leslie had to turn to the very Saviour he preached about for the same grace that saves, delivers and restores the soul.

Yes, the bitter experience changed his life and hurt his closest relationships, but 'that fire' never went out! As the inner fire slowly re-ignited, Bill gradually began to shine with even deeper sensitivity and passion to minister the love of Christ.

Be blessed and challenged as you read this birds-eye view of a man God used for His Glory.

**"Down in the human heart crushed by the tempter,
Feelings lie buried that grace can
restore. Touched by a loving hand,
wakened by kindness
Chords that were broken shall vibrate once more"**
- Fanny Crosby

CONTENTS

Section 1. New Beginnings

- ***It took a Miracle***

Chapter 1. St. Mary's

Chapter 2. Tom Crocker

Chapter 3. Days of Decision

Section 2 - Officership

- ***Doing the will of God***

Chapter 4. Lieut. Leslie

Chapter 5. Sherbourne Street

Chapter 6. Realized Dream

Section 3 -

Miracle Years

- **God can do anything**

Chapter 7. Powell Street Miracles
Chapter 8. Cordova Street Miracles
Chapter 9. Miracles of Grace

Chapter 10. Miracle Valley
Chapter 11. The Last Brigadier

Section 4

- **You can start over again**

Chapter 12. Geographical cures
Chapter 13. Fernie House
Chapter 14. Missions and Miracles
Chapter 15. Final Promotion

Dedicated to the Harbour Lighters

- Officers, Staff, and Supporters:

Men and women who had a passion for the lost and who followed the call to
"Go for souls and go for the worst."
(William Booth)

Section 1 - New Beginnings

"It took a miracle to put the
stars in place, It took a miracle
to hang the world in space; But
when He saved my soul,
Cleansed and made me whole,
It took a miracle of love and grace."

- John W. Peterson

Copyright 1948, Renewal 1978 by John W. Peterson Music Company

Chapter 1 – St. Mary's

'The Stone Town' it is called. Layers of limestone and rock form its foundation where it sits along the banks of Southern Ontario's meandering Thames River. The town's real name, St. Mary's, is situated about half way between Stratford in the north and London in the south, amidst road and rail transportation links, lush lands and abundant water supplies. Municipal edifices constructed from the locally-quarried rock boast magnificence like many of the stone buildings in Southwest Ontario. St. Mary's also boasts the largest natural swimming pool in Ontario, compliments of quarry #1, and is home to the huge and productive St. Mary's Cement Company.

Immigrants flocking to this desirable haven included the Leslie clan from Scotland in the 1800's. They began as farmers but irrigation projects forced many into the town proper where Earl Leslie, born in the late 19th century, was raised with a very strict Catholic upbringing. Young Earl fell in love with and married (Feb. 24, 1918) Ruth Skipper, a Protestant, and was immediately disowned by his family. Undeterred, young and strong, Earl encountered no difficulty in finding work in the limestone quarries and later in the cement plant.

Ruth was raised in a British family which, in their London, England, home, had embraced the teachings and convictions of William Booth, Founder of the Salvation Army. The Skippers proudly wore Salvation Army uniforms and supported the local Corps (church), much to the dismay of Earl's staunchly Catholic family.

Earl and Ruth, settled into a small, comfortable home situated a few blocks south of the St. Mary's railway station and in 1919 welcomed their first child, Douglas. Douglas lived barely two years before succumbing to the fatal effects of flu. Dorothy, born

in 1922, was followed by a brother, William, May 24, 1925.

Four more girls, Kathleen, Ruth, Grace and Helen, then two boys, Jack and Don, rounded out the family unit. William, who was dubbed 'Bill', lived a happy and care-free life until the decade-long Great Depression of 1929.

Employment was extremely hard to come by. Hard-working Earl maintained employment at the cement plant but the pay could not keep pace with the needs of a growing family. Survival meant everyone had to pitch in: children worked in the family garden, fished for perch in the river, and foraged for coal along the railway tracks. The coal hoppers, manned by friendly engineers on the locomotives, seemed to be forever 'losing' coal as they daily screeched their way through town. Bill raised money from the local golf course where he found and sold 'lost' golf balls, a skill which never left him. In later years, golfing companions would be frustrated by Bill spending too much time in the rough earnestly searching for those little white orbs. On the plus side, golfing buddies would return home with more golf balls than they had taken to the course!

Bill, an apt and intelligent student excelling in hockey and boxing, felt the pressures of adolescence in wanting to help support the family. Age 13, he quit school at the end of Grade 8 and left home seeking work. Big for his age with a rugged, athletic body, he found a job at a foundry in Hespler (now Cambridge, Ontario) an hour's distance from home, as an apprentice moulder. He journeyed home as often as he could, added regularly to the family's finances and kept up with his athletic endeavors as much as he was able. As a vulnerable teen working closely with men three or four times his age, Bill was easily drawn into drinking with 'the boys' in the Silver Dollar Hotel at the close of each shift. Training ended after only a year so the employer could look for another apprentice in order to maintain cheaper labour. It was the start of Bill's drifting days.

Chapter 2 – Tom Crocker

It was a year pivotal in world history - 1939. Germany had re- militarized in the West while Japan, in the East, declared itself an Imperial power. Wars and rumours of war flourished creating
massive global unease: Canada's economy was still weak and working conditions tenuous. Bill Leslie urgently plied the corridor between London and Toronto looking for any type of work he could obtain. The next two years saw him take employment in the 'gig' economy, long before the Millennials would popularize the phrase to describe short-term, part-time jobs. He kept being drawn back to Toronto where he had established friendships with others just like himself, young, restless, and eager to prove themselves in their world. Toronto's Queen Street, and the dark areas around it, became his favourite haunt. And haunted he was as his lifestyle degenerated from the truths he had learned at his mother's knee.

"I thank God for a dear, Christian mother who prayed for me. She would write to me, and on each page the ink on the paper would be blurred with tears as she pleaded with me to get right with the Lord," Leslie later confessed.

As Bill daily hunted significant employment, another man, also struggling with inner turmoil and fighting life's demons, was to significantly impact Bill's life.

It was October 7, 1939, a cold, moonless night in a downtown Detroit park. The bitter, freezing wind blasted Tom Crocker into full wakefulness as an attack of the 'jimmies', the D T's (delirium tremens) overtook his bruised and battered body. His legs would barely move. The pain that struck him as he attempted to stand was overwhelming. Desperate with fear and hunger, Tom aimed his broken body in the direction of the Salvation Army Bowery hall in the city's economically-battered Skid Row area. Staggering and stumbling with every awkward, painful step he lurched inside and literally collapsed into a seat.

"Someone was speaking. I couldn't even make out what he

looked like let alone what he was saying," Tom later related. "All I knew was that I longed for him to finish soon. I just ached for a bowl of hot soup; that was all I could think of. Then, I don't know where it came from, my mind suddenly became clear and I heard the man say something about 'coming forward' and 'being saved'. Dragging myself to my feet I staggered down the aisle, fell in front of the man, pleading as I looked up into his face, 'Do you think your Jesus could save me?'"

"Give Him a chance," the wise and Godly man responded. "I began to cry and told my story to Jesus that night. They put me in a real, warm bed in the dormitory of the Bowery Corps."

For two days Crocker remained in bed until things began to become more peaceful in his mind and body until he was able to sleep again - eat regularly, and began to think clear, sensible thoughts. From that time forward Tom Crocker never again touched tobacco, booze or drugs! It took a mighty miracle to bring Tom back to a place of dignity in society: a miracle was needed because his life had been lost in the skids for twenty years.

Thomas A. Crocker started life in 1894, one of five children in a family of middle income. His father died when Tom was 17 so he quit school and went to work. Not much later he joined the Navy and served on an escort ship convoying cargo and troops across the Atlantic until the end of W.W.1.

Upon demobilization, Tom tried politics and became a court clerk. He had a quick intellect and the gift of a silver tongue. "I began to drink a little at first," he confessed, "and then more heavily. I had a good Christian mother but I refused to listen to her as she tried to persuade me to give up the drink."

The craving for alcohol cost Crocker his court job and every other job thereafter. Repeatedly hospitalized while coming off drinking binges, he was given morphine to quiet his nerves and then the morphine got him. Addictions drew him into a downward spiral until he was an unrecognizable denizen of skid row. For eight long, hard years he daily shuffled around the worst areas of his home town.

Jesus saved Tom Crocker on that frigid October night. For the next two years Tom couldn't keep from working and witnessing, urgently trying to persuade his buddies on the street to get their lives changed too. The Salvation Army realized they had a

dynamic 'new creation' on their hands. In 1941 Tom, commissioned as a Salvation Army Captain, took command of the Bowery Corps and was to begin a new project out of that centre in Detroit, to develop a dedicated service for the addicted.

Tom spent the next 17 years developing and initiating the Harbour Light work in Detroit, Chicago and Los Angeles. In 1954 he received the Army's highest honour - The Order of The Founder - named for General William Booth who founded The Salvation Army in 1865. In May 1959, Captain Tom Crocker, O.F., was 'Promoted to Glory'.

Of his passing the Chicago Tribune had this to say: "Thousands of self-respecting citizens all over America felt pangs of deep sorrow when they heard of the death of that man in uniform. He was Captain Thomas A. Crocker, 64, former drunkard, former morphine addict, former forger, who once lifted those stalwart citizens out of Skid Row."

Chapter 3 – Days of Decision

Skid Row, Bourbon Street, Asphalt Jungle, the Bowery, or Unknown City; every city has such an area be it a single street or a designated neighborhood. Life is cheap there; dreams end and every sort of commodity is sold so that anyone can obtain the chemical(s) they crave, from the finest bottled liquor to 'canned heat', also known as 'Pink Lady'. (Recipe: squeeze a can of Sterno jelly through cheesecloth or a pair of used socks and mix the solution with soda pop. Cream soda is best for colour match. Drink. Result? Oblivion, temporary loss of caring about anything, inability to face reality as the drug leaves the body, possible blindness, insatiable desire for more and more and . . .). Drugs can be ingested, snorted, smoked or injected; the choice is irrelevant so long as a state of oblivion is reached - that state where life's disappointments, abuses, mistakes, guilt, fears and losses are wiped away.

For Bill Leslie, two very dark years saw him taste the life of horror-ridden streets. 'Someday Street is a one-way street that heads to the gates of Hell' are the words poet Buekert had penned from his own bitter experience. Nights of blackouts, waking buck naked in a city park, sporting cuts and bruises from some brawl engaged in, all ran together in clouded unreality. Trips home to St. Mary's had become less and less frequent, and were mainly only to keep up with his love of boxing, too ashamed to spend much time around the house.

In Canada, economically things were looking up. War production was now in full swing and Bill landed a job at one of the big steel mills in Hamilton. With apprenticeship finally paying off, Bill's skill was valued and he was proud to take part in the war effort, pouring molds for aircraft parts. For the next two years he kept his nose pretty clean while working shifts, regularly drinking with local pals and winning (albeit infrequently) a few dollars from playing craps. Still one of the youngest guys on the crew, Bill had grown to his full height of 5′ 10″, and was in fighting form with a barrel chest and well-muscled arms.

It was 1943. Bill had just turned 18. Seeking to do his part in fighting for his country, he presented himself to the Navy Recruiting Centre; Navy because he loved the dark uniforms of Navy personnel. He filled out the endless, essential forms, showed his I.D. to the clerk, and waited. The medical check-up doctor, quick and efficient, informed Bill that he had failed the medical.

"Ridiculous! I'm in the best shape of my life," the exasperated Leslie shouted. "You're in great shape, fella, but you've got the worst case of colour-blindness that I've ever seen," announced the physician. To add insult to injury, the waiting room clerk officiously informed Bill that the armed forces could not accept him because his current job was deemed an essential service.

Rejected, the dejected young man hit the bars that night to drown his disappointment. Oblivion, the siren call of the streets, would be Bill's desire for months ahead. Stubbornness and pride kept him from abandoning himself to the seductive voice of hedonism but he was bitter and angry, feeling that his only value was that of an 'essential worker'. At the close of each work-day's shift he quickly submerged himself in the relentless, unfeeling street life, seeking diversion, anything to fill the emptiness of his soul.

On a late September evening in 1943, while aimlessly wandering yet again around the streets of East Toronto, Bill's ears picked up the sound of songs he hadn't heard for years. He followed the music of the marching Salvation Army brass band to the Brock Avenue Corps (church) and was curiously drawn in by the warmth and light to listen further. The speaker on the platform was the Corps Officer, Captain Leslie Pindred, one of the Army's finest evangelists. That simple Gospel message spoke directly to Bill Leslie and stirred something deep within his hurting heart. As the message came to a close, an invitation was offered to anyone who wanted to give up inner fighting and to place one's heartfelt trust in

Jesus. Bill hesitatingly stood, stumbled to the Mercy Seat, a wooden bench at the front of the building, and, in front of a church-full of people, humbly knelt, sincerely sought forgiveness, and prayerfully gave his heart to the Lord. That seemingly interminable emptiness of his soul was immediately filled withincredible joy. His mother's prayers were answered!

"Hey, guys," Bill announced to his foundry workmates the following day, "something happened to me at The Salvation Army last night. I got saved!" The resultant jeers and laughter of his work buddies did not discourage him and he convinced one of the gang to go with him to the Army service that night. All afternoon he prayed for his buddy, and that evening his friend was kneeling at that same mercy seat, getting *his* heart right with Jesus. Life dramatically changed. Instead of drinking and playing craps at the foundry work place, the two men read the New Testaments given to them by Capt. Pindred. These two young, brand-new converts talked to a girl who worked in the company office and she went with them to the Salvation Army Corps and got saved also. The following Friday, she brought her boyfriend along and sure enough, he too got saved! This was the thrilling miracle of Bill Leslie's baby steps as a 'new creation' in Christ Jesus.

The following year, Bill attended a Salvation Army youth rally in downtown Toronto. Above the platform a large banner read: 'Young men and women wanted as Salvation Army Officers.' Again, he felt a strange stirring in his heart and knew that this was the purpose in life he was meant to pursue. To obtain release from what was deemed an 'essential service' position in his place of employment during the war years was considered an impossibility, but Leslie, along with the support of Capt. Pindred, completed the application and after only a mere nine months as a newborn Christian, he was released from work and accepted for the 1944-45 Session of Canada's Salvation Army Training College for Officers in Toronto.

During his time as a cadet (a trainee), Bill, along with other cadets, was sent to conduct meetings in Detroit at the Bowery Corps where Bill met that amazing 'trophy of grace', Capt. Tom Crocker. Leslie actually billeted with Crocker for the weekend. Again his heart was deeply stirred.

"What an experience!" Bill later exclaimed. "God told me plainly 'this is My plan for your life.'" He reluctantly returned to Toronto but, every Friday afternoon ('free time' from college studies) for the rest of his year-long training days, Bill would travel down to Toronto's Skid Row area to speak with and counsel men trapped in the horrific street life.

College studies brought education in Bible and doctrinal studies, Salvation Army procedures, the art of preaching, and practical leadership training. Music was a huge factor for Bill while in the College on Davisville Avenue after it was discovered that he had a rich baritone voice and a keen ear for music. A cornet was thrust into his hands and he quickly began to correctly finger tunes though he never learned to read a note of music. "Musicians learn the keys and notes," Leslie quipped. "I learned by letter. I just open my mouth and 'let 'er rip'!" He could memorize though, and readily copied the fingering of the player beside him as long as they were playing the melody. And he learned to play the bass fiddle, lugging that awkward, heavy wooden instrument to open- air street meetings wherever his College brigade (team) was sent to minister.

He had been carefully discipled by Capt. Pindred prior to becoming a Cadet and the Captain had discovered two things about then Candidate Leslie; one, he was a natural evangelist, and two, he was blessed with a phenomenal capacity to memorize. A memory tool Pindred challenged Bill with was a 'Promise Box' with 100 pieces of cardboard chips each with a Scripture verse on one side and a poem or thought on the other. Bill easily memorized those 100 Scriptures in less than six months. Later he would commit chapters and whole books of the Bible to memory, building a solid foundation for future ministry.

"Do your studying and learning while you're young," Leslie proclaimed many times later in life. "Life becomes too busy and it is important that a Scriptural foundation is laid while you can."

William Ronald Leslie, upon graduation from The Salvation Army College for Officers, was commissioned as a Probationary Lieutenant, appointed to assist at the Parliament Street Corps in the section of Toronto affectionately, or scornfully, known as 'Cabbage Town'.

Section 2 - Officership

"Doing the will of God
Doing the will of God,
The best thing I know in this world below is
Doing the will of God. "

Chapter 4 – Lieut. Leslie

Lieutenant Leslie, settling into his first 'appointment' at Parliament Street Corps, immediately found a new friend and mentor in his Commanding Officer, Capt. Vic Greenwood. Like Bill, Vic had a passion for the lost and immediately agreed they should create a soup line operating out of the Corps building. Their rickety 1929 Pontiac car chugged around Moss Park (the center of Skid Row) to pick up any hungry derelicts, transport them to the Army hall for a nutritious dinner and a red-hot Gospel meeting. Many, many men found themselves kneeling at the Mercy Seat, seeking God's forgiveness and receiving salvation by the end of each service.

One such notable convert was Teddy Horner. Teddy, just released from jail, was found cowering in a back alley behind Queen Street, in terrible shape both physically and mentally. Horner was one of those men who accepted the invitation to humbly kneel at the Mercy Seat and received Jesus as his Saviour. Once recovered in body and spirit he soon became a respected citizen of the community. Within months he was enrolled as a 'soldier' (Salvation Army term for 'member') at the Parliament

Street Corps, and progressed in his business life to become a valued employee of a local bank.

It would be typical of Bill Leslie to celebrate each salvation event by having others join the baritone voice emerging from deep within his chest, to sing, as he did hundreds, perhaps thousands of times over the years:

> **"It is no secret, what God can do. What He's done for others, He'll do for you. With arms wide open, He'll pardon you. It is no secret, what God can do."** (Stuart Hamblen)

Farewell Orders! 'Orders' emanate from The Salvation Army's Divisional or Territorial Headquarters. Serving for only one year as an Officer at Parliament Street Corps, Lieutenant Leslie received 'farewell orders' then subsequent 'marching orders' and was appointed to take charge of the Army's work in Haliburton, Ontario. The magnificent countryside of the Haliburton highlands was enjoyed only briefly as the snow and arctic conditions of Northern Ontario

embraced Bill's new home by Thanksgiving, October, '46. Bill quickly adjusted to his new role as Commanding Officer. The small Army hall soon proved to be inadequate to hold the ever-increasing crowds attending the evening Salvation meetings. Permission was secured to use the larger premises of the local Baptist church on Sunday evenings and God truly blessed the ministry with expanding numbers. Somewhere along the way, Bill obtained a banjo and quickly learned the trick of
fingering the strings to play a 'G' chord. He skillfully began the rhythmical strum of the three basic chords of most Gospel songs and was soon wearing the title "Banjo" Bill. Though encouraged by the growth of the Corps, Bill still had a deep longing in his heart to minister to the men on the streets of Toronto. He wrote to the Officer in charge of Canada's Salvation Army's Officer appointments, the Field Secretary, expressing his experiences and desire. The reply was not encouraging. Bill was reminded that it was his duty to keep on praying and that the leaders of the Army were quite capable of

knowing where its officers should be stationed.

"I prayed and prayed," Bill said, "but the burden on my heart only increased. Finally I left the Corps appointment of my own accord, giving headquarters adequate time to appoint another Officer in my place." Tom Crocker, hearing of Bill's predicament, invited him to the U.S.A. to assist in starting a new work in Chicago. It was to be the Army's first custom-developed, holistic treatment centre for the addicted - the Harbour Light. Remembering that earlier
visit, Leslie recounted, "I jumped at the chance and stayed with Tom for six months, assisting him in opening that centre on Madison Avenue. Oh, to be working with such a saintly, Spirit- filled man! I thank God for every moment I worked with him- what a blessed privilege."

Tom Crocker had not only experienced what it was to lose everything in life and spend years living on Skid Row, he had also been subjected to almost every known alcohol and drug treatment of that time. He wisely developed a program utilizing psychological, compassionate best practices along with a strong spiritual component to encourage not only the outer man, but also the inner man to be transformed. Captain Tom, upon being questioned about his success in rehabilitating men would reply, "I am not interested in the theology of what has happened or the psychology of it; I just want to help a man find God and realize that, in Him, he can start new life."

Despite repeated requests by Lieutenant Leslie to be transferred from Canada to The Salvation Army U.S.A. Central Territory, he was ordered, in true military fashion, to report back to Toronto by the end of the year (1947) or his Officership would be terminated. Bill reluctantly obeyed the command and was sorely disappointed he was not free to participate in the Grand Opening of the Chicago Harbour Light in January, 1948. Bill did find however, that the Lord had prepared a period of fulfilling ministry, and even romance, in his new appointment at the Sherbourne Street Hostel for Men in Toronto.

Chapter 5 – Sherbourne Street

It is an old, red-brick building standing proudly at Toronto's  Sherbourne and Queen Street intersection, originally built as the Salvation Army's Training College for Officers. In 1915 the College was moved to a locale on Davisville Avenue, North Toronto, and the Sherbourne Street site was renovated as a hostel for workingmen. (Sherbourne Street is one of the original streets in the old city of York, Upper Canada. The Hostel is now known as the Maxwell Meighen Centre.) During the frightening Depression years the building was again renovated and many of the single rooms were transformed into cubicles and dormitories designed for destitute men living on the streets. When Bill Leslie, the new Assistant Officer took up the appointment in 1948, the Hostel had the capacity to accommodate and to minister to 250 men.

"I went under the direction of the Holy Spirit," Leslie later remembered, "and during the next four and one-half years we saw an increase in services to the poor and many souls won for Christ. Several of the converts went on to be commissioned as Salvation Army Officers. Two of these men, Bill Bird and James McCready, would later assist me with the work in Vancouver. "

James McCready migrated to Canada from Ireland when only 22. During WWII he had served with the Canadian army through many of the major campaigns as a munitions truck driver, a bitter experience that left him a broken man, unable to cope with the horrors endured. It was a bottom-of-the barrel day when James shuffled along Sherbourne Street heading for the Toronto docks where he intended to end his own life. Drowning in misery, he was unexpectedly drawn by bright music drifting from the chapel at the Salvation Army Hostel. Like so many before him, James found himself kneeling at the Mercy Seat pouring out his story to Lieutenant Leslie. As a new man, given time, he joined the staff at the hostel where he later met and married his wife, Hannah, in 1949, and both were commissioned as Officers in the Salvation Army.

In 1948 Bill was destined to meet his greatest help-mate at an official gathering of Salvation Army Officers in Toronto. Captain Mildred Williamson, an Officer-Nurse stationed at Toronto's Grace hospital, caught Bill's fancy. With a huge grin on his face and a flashing twinkle in his eye, Bill swept Mildred of her feet and wed her on May 14, 1949.

Wedding Day 1949

Mildred Ester Williamson was born on Feb. 27, 1922 in Little Current on Manitoulin Island, Ontario. She had an older brother (Albert), two younger sisters (Doris and Helen), and three younger brothers (Bob, Jim and Joe). Her father was a dredgerman, keeping the harbours of the island from silting up, while her mother was kept busy with the large family. Mildred remembered accepting Jesus as her Saviour as a child in the old Baptist church where the kids attended Sunday school. When The Salvation Army 'opened fire' in Little Current in the mid-30's, Mildred and her sister were drawn in by the vibrant brass band music and the lively fellowship of the Army's youth group.

Graduated from high school, Mildred volunteered to do her part in the war effort by leaving home to work in the General Electric plant in Peterborough, Ont. She signed up as a soldier in the

Peterborough Salvation Army Corps, responded to the persuasive inner call to Officership, then, following training in Toronto's Officer's College 'Valiant' session (1942-43), was commissioned as a Lieutenant in charge of the Corps in Kingsville, Ontario. A year later she was re-appointed to receive training as an Officer- Nurse at The Salvation Army's Grace Hospital in Windsor, Ontario. Mildred's nursing skills quickly led to the role of Nurse Instructor before being re-appointed again (1947), this time to Toronto Grace Hospital where she served as a nurse until her marriage to Bill Leslie.

The Leslies lived peacefully in a second-floor apartment in the Sherbourne Street Hostel. Mildred's calm and quiet manner served to bring balance to Bill's high-energy life. She became a bookkeeper for the Hostel and her many nursing skills were often called upon as men arrived at the hostel with a multitude of ailments that required her efficient, gentle care.

The clamor of unbelievably deafening horns and screaming sirens rudely awakened Bill and Mildred at 2:30 a.m. It was one of the worst disasters in Toronto's history, Sept. 17, 1949. The S.S. Noronic, a Great Lakes Luxury Cruise Liner

Photo – Toronto Daily Star, Sept.17, 1949

berthed a few blocks south at Pier 9, was engulfed in a raging fire with 524 passengers on board, plus the crew. The fire was so swift, and the heat so intense that no-one other than the fire-fighting crew was able to approach the inferno.

As one of the Army centres closest to the disaster, the resident Officers and staff of the Hostel were on full alert for 3 hours before being allowed to assist with sandwiches and refreshments for the first responders. Bill was immediately assigned work on the dock assisting with rescue and retrieval efforts. Mildred ably nursed those in medical need at the makeshift triage. The Salvation Army was asked to provide counsel to the surviving victims and to families of the 119 deceased. Many bodies, greatly ravaged by fire, had to be identified by what was then a new forensic technique, identification by dental records. One of the Salvation Army's unofficial mottos was 'Ready For Anything', indicating there are some things that one never wants to have to be prepared for. The tragic and deadly 'Noronic' fire was one of those horrific events.

As the next two and a half years flew by, staff at the Hostel accomplished something remarkably unusual. A fully functioning Corps (a church, which should be officially under the headship of The Salvation Army *Field* Department) was operating in a Men's Social Service facility, (officially headed by The Salvation Army *Social Services* Department.) There were so many folk being saved and becoming enrolled as soldiers, not to mention those being sent to Officer's Training College, that the Hostel became an outpost (satellite church) of the Parliament Street Corps. The number one baby dedication recorded on the rolls of that outpost Corps was the firstborn son of Bill and Mildred Leslie, William Paul Leslie, born December 30, 1950.

Chapter 6 - Realized Dream

Blessings in abundance, a bustling ministry at hand, yet still Bill Leslie was yearning for more as his vision of a dedicated outreach and treatment program for the addicted had not been realized. A Harbour Light Centre in Toronto's Skid Row was what he dreamed of and schemed for. His conception of how the dream could be realized arose in 1952 when the perfect property became available, just around the corner from the Sherbourne Street Hostel, in the late spring of 1952. If an established Corps could operate inside the Social Services Department, why could a Harbour Light Corps not operate in the same way? He painstakingly developed a plan for how the Hostel and the desired new ministry could work together to support one another. The plan was scrupulously presented to Army superiors, the property rented, then Leslie was told to wait while renovations took place. The windows of the Queen Street site were soon covered to conceal the work inside and construction crews were observed entering the building.

Weeks of frustrating silence! Bill reached out to the Men's Social Services administration to seek information about the renovations and to ask if he could aid in the architectural and program planning. The response was devastating! The project plan had been dramatically changed so that the property was no longer slated to be a Harbour Light Centre, but would become a fine Thrift Store.

Bill was staggered! In his anger he vowed to never hold an appointment in the Men's Social Services Department again. He immediately requested a meeting with Canada's Territorial Commander to demand an explanation and to determine whether the Army in Canada would ever contemplate beginning a Harbour Light ministry. In June, 1952, Captain Leslie had his meeting at Territorial Headquarters with Commissioner Wm. R. Dalziel.

Dalziel, a formidable man, a commanding figure, was feared as well as respected. Big in physique, apt in leadership, he had served the Army in Canada both as

Chief Secretary and now as Territorial Commander (the highest position an Officer can attain in the Canadian Territory). He also had a big heart and listened intently as Bill Leslie poured out his story of genuine passion for the lost. Dalziel promised; as soon as opportunity arose Bill would be given the task of starting a Harbour Light in Canada. Meanwhile, the Leslie's were transferred to take charge of the Long Branch Corps in the Toronto Division.

For ten long months Leslie wrested with God about his life and future. As he prayed he absorbed a brief poem by C.T. Studd, a 19th century reformer and a contemporary of William Booth, founder of The world-wide Salvation Army. The words encapsulated Bill's passion:

"Some want to live within the sound of church or chapel bell. I want to run a rescue shop within a yard of hell."

The interminably-long waiting days were not without benefit.

Bill, with time away from the demanding pressures of helping to administrate a large institution, took valuable opportunity to reflect on and ingest God's word, and was thrilled to welcome a new life into his and Mildred's world: Ruth Anne Leslie, their first daughter, was born on Sept. 13, 1952.

The telephone rang unusually loud in the Officer's quarters in Long Branch on April 23, 1953. The caller advised Captain Leslie to report to the Territorial Commander's office at Territorial Headquarters. Bill drove his car from the western boundaries of Toronto to the downtown Jarvis Street offices with no idea of what lay ahead. Had he known, he would surely have accumulated speeding tickets along the way. Commissioner Dalziel was very much aware his news needed to be delivered as soon as possible to the restless, dynamic young Officer - the usual written 'marching orders' would not suffice.

"You are appointed to go and open a Harbour Light Corps in the city of Vancouver," Dalziel pronounced to the startled Leslie. "There's a small work already going on there. Make it or break it!" The welcome announcement was a prelude to a series of miracles! Practical arrangements were started immediately. Bill was to proceed to Vancouver to 'scout out the land 'and see what the present, fledgling ministry was like. Mildred would stay on to look after the kids and manage the Long Branch Corps until a replacement Officer could be appointed. On May 3, 1953, an excited Captain Bill Leslie and an eager Sergeant Mike McNeil (a willing volunteer from the Sherbourne Street Hostel) arrived in the west coast port city of Vancouver, British Columbia.

Section 3 - Miracle Years

"God can do anything, anything,
anything, God can do anything but fail
God can do anything, anything, anything
God can do anything but fail
He's the Alpha and Omega, the beginning and the end
He's the fairest of ten thousand to my soul
God can do anything, anything, anything
God can do anything but fail
He can save, He can
cleanse He can keep, and
He will God can do
anything but fail He can
save, He can cleanse He
can keep, and He will God
can do anything but fail"

- Ira F. Stanphill

Chapter 7 - Powell Street Miracles

The exciting, adventurous story of the Army marching into Western Canada is recorded in 'The Blood and Fire in Canada: A history of the Salvation Army in the Dominion 1882-1976' (R.G. Moyles). Since 1887 'Bonnets and Bands' had been evident in Vancouver but by 1952 the metropolis had dire need to find an effective means of alleviating the suffering of the ever-increasing numbers of alcoholics in its expanding Skid Row.

Harbour Light's humble beginnings at 55A Powell Street

Major David and Mrs. Hammond® had visited Captain Tom Crocker in Detroit, spring '52, to observe the Harbour Light ministry pioneered by Tom. Moved with genuine compassion for the plight of the desperate men and women on Skid Row, the Hammonds dreamed of a similar centre in Vancouver. With the encouragement of Brigadier Charles Watt, Commanding Officer Vancouver Temple Corps, and the support of retired Corps Sergeant- Major George Hodson, it was in August that the Hammonds were able to rent a small, temporary facility at 55A Powell

Street, the former O.K. Smoke Shop situated in the dark heart of Skid Row. From this dingy, tiny store with its single washroom, a miniscule office and a room barely capable of seating 25 people wedged closely together, Gospel meetings with coffee and buns became the catalyst to a future that was almost unimaginable. The months of time, labour, and groundwork given by those early faithful witnesses were rewarded!

Captain and Mrs. Leslie, appointed by Headquarters to establish a Harbour Light ministry in the busy port city of Vancouver, began to build on that humble foundation. The cheerless, ex-bookie joint that had more telephone wires than light fixtures, the O.K. Smoke Shop, soon furnished with a few folding chairs and an old coffee percolator, was the beginning of the expansion of operations under Capt. Leslie and assistant Sgt. Mike McNeil. A couple of used army cots, a two-burner Coleman stove and a few food supplies were acquired with a loan of one hundred dollars from the local Household Finance Company. That's how it began – the critical ministry of outreach to the harshest, darkest streets of the city.

With a Banjo hanging around his neck, a Bible in one hand while stirring rich-smelling stew on the Coleman stove with the other, night after night, Monday through Friday, Bill preached an urgent message of everlasting love, salvation and freedom to restless men crammed shoulder to shoulder on uncomfortable folding chairs. Mike's job was to warmly welcome the somewhat disorderly men stumbling in from the street. Weekends were predominantly taken up with sharing the vision of a Harbour Light ministry at area Salvation Army Corps and other churches, and asking for help in realizing that dream.

Almost immediately the search was on to locate a more suitable property in the downtown area, a facility that would provide a proper kitchen, space for at least 20 beds, a meeting/dining area for at least 100 persons, washrooms, storage and office areas.

Within two months just the right property as found: a new 'For Sale' sign was displayed at 56 Powell, directly across the street from the Smoke Shop! It was a decrepit, old hotel operation that had gone bankrupt. Perfect! Square footage was ideal and the building could be renovated to meet the requirements of a Harbour Light centre.

> "It was in the early 1950's and my friend, Bill, was pioneering a program for alcoholics. "Come with me," he invited, and we went to a place in the city's skid row, a vacant building Bill thought could become a rehabilitation centre. It had been a beer parlor, then a machine shop,

and evidence of both former uses were there, though barely visible because the windows had become so covered with grime. We knelt between the rusty tractor treads and pieces of broken chain, and began to pray. Something in Bill's tone gripped me; I could not refrain from opening my eyes. He was reaching up and looking up. Tears streamed as he pled, "O God, for the salvation of the men here who need you, give me this place." There was emotion in it, so much so that the scene is, for me, quite unforgettable. But more than mere emotion, there was faith in that prayer, and love for the lost. Hundreds, perhaps thousands, were later to come to Christ at that very spot."
Timothy My Son. Ed Read.

After Bill's former unhappy experience with the proposed Toronto Sherbourne Street building, oversight of the renovations were carefully monitored by the now more-experienced Captain Leslie.

With two children in tow, Mildred arrived in Vancouver from Toronto in July. Bill had rented a 2- bedroom basement suite on the east side of Vancouver that was home until 1955 when the old 'quarters' (Officer's house) of the East Vancouver Grandview Corps became vacant. Once settled into their new surroundings

Mildred became involved with the ministry on Powell Street. Since Bill was adept at raising funds but not so much at handling them, Mildred served as bookkeeper for the rapidly growing Harbour Light.

Renovations to the new Harbour Light Centre were visibly advancing daily. Bill not only raised funds, but had tapped into ready and willing volunteer resources. Those welcome volunteers, along with men with long-dormant skills, now recovering from life on the streets, hammered, nailed, sawed and painted the main floor of 56 Powell creating a Chapel/Dining hall able to seat and feed 120 men. Behind that hall they rebuilt a kitchen, washrooms and office space. Completed renovations on the upper floor would accommodate up to 22 men.

By the grace of God, along with a score of prayer warriors and volunteers, the Leslies had built on, not 'broken', as some sadly negative folk voiced, that faith-inspired work of the Hammonds. September 15, 1953 Commissioner Dalziel, following protocol, confirmed the opening of the new Harbour Light Corps. October 1st of that same year, Dalziel personally flew from Toronto Headquarters to Vancouver to officially open and dedicate the newly-renovated building at 56 Powell Street.

The only regret in all of this miraculous work was that Senior Major David Hammond® had been 'Promoted to Glory' before seeing the exciting official opening of the work he had tirelessly begun. (Or, perhaps he had the 'best seat in the house'!)

A year flew by. Outreach meetings with meals, were held twice a day, Monday to Saturday. Sunday mornings featured a Holiness meeting for the converts and adherents of the Harbour Light, followed with the usual Salvation Army evangelistic outreach in the evening. The First Anniversary service took place September 1954. Well-known city jeweller, David Firbank, (Firbank's Jewellers) told the audience: "You fellows could turn Vancouver upside down." He noted that the Harbour Light, in its first year of operation, had already seen staggering success figures: 414 men asked the Lord to save them, 893 were helped to obtainemployment, 967 were provided with free beds, 75,018 free meals were served, and 76,571 persons attended services where they heard the Gospel offered. That Christmas, the Harbour Light served its first of many Christmas dinners, open to all on the street who wished to dine. The 'full meal deal', a sit-down turkey dinner with all the trimmings, was shared by 525 homeless men, each of whom received a small gift of candies, mixed nuts, and a pair of new socks. Expressions of Gratitude were enormous!

How could anyone feed all those people? It took faith in God, Jehovah-Jireh (the God who provides), plus willing, great chefs. Leslie found such a one in Fred Chapman. Fred had once been an executive chef at the King Edward Hotel in Toronto. Alcohol led to his downfall and, literally down and out, Fred arrived defeated and broken on the doorsteps of the Sherbourne Street hostel. It was there that he met Bill Leslie, received Jesus Christas his Saviour and within a few months was
serving on staff as a cook at the hostel. Capt. Leslie called Fred in Toronto, September,1953, to assist in the

ground- breaking work of the new Harbour Light. Food was often in short supply but God's provision was often miraculous.

On one occasion, shortly after 56 Powell was opened, Bill called the converts and volunteers together to do what was fast becoming the most normal thing to do - Pray! The larder was emptying out quickly and needed to be filled if hungry men were to eat. Those prayers were answered in a most peculiar way. The newly opened Safeway Grocery and Produce store at Victoria Drive and 41st Avenue was operational for only a few weeks when disaster struck a fire ravaged the store! 60,000 tins of canned goods survived the blaze with only minor water and smoke damage to the tins. The store manager, Joe Hicks, phoned Capt. Leslie offering him the entire stock of canned foods for free! They just had to be picked up. Chef Chapman was delighted to be able to prepare more than just the customary soup or stew.

56 Powell Street, which had initially seemed so spacious with its extensive renovations, was now proving to be woefully inadequate. The Corps history book recorded, July, 1955: "After many months of earnest prayer we made a purchase offer for our proposed new building at the corner of Columbia and Cordova Streets." The edifice was the El

Rancho Hotel at 119 East Cordova Street, an old building of ill repute but it was at least twice the size of the current building. Possession of the El Rancho took place in March, 1956 and extensive renovations rattled the downtown Skid Row area for the next seven months. Leslie and his workers prayed earnestly and laboured almost daily to meet the grand opening and dedication date set for October 13, 1956.

As the Harbour Light ministry grew and flourished so did the Leslie family with the November 20, 1955 birth of their 2nd daughter, Kathleen Esther Leslie.

Chapter 8 – Cordova Street Miracles

Newly plastered walls demand hot air to dry. Noisy, hot-air gas fans, operating day and night for several weeks demand many dollars. Renovations were being rushed in order to have the Cordova Street location ready for an Oct. 13th opening: the resulting cost was an exorbitant $500. (To show relativity, this was at a time when houses in the Vancouver market cost less than $10,000.)

The day the bill was received, Leslie called together the men on the rehabilitation program for a special prayer meeting in the newly finished 200-seat chapel. They prayed, earnestly asking the Lord for $500 to pay for the extraordinary expense. That very afternoon a letter arrived in the mail from a "little old lady" (Leslie's words) living in West Vancouver, with a cheque enclosed in the amount of $500! That answer to prayer was just one of many similar miracles to occur in the lifetime of the 'Rescue Shop'.

One of the first residents of 119 East Cordova was not an alcoholic but a young, starving artist with nowhere to live. He had a deal for

Bill Leslie; in exchange for board and room the artist would create a fitting scene for the wall of the newly constructed chapel. He laboured on his painting project for weeks and, upon completion, the beautiful art work blanketed most of the rear wall of the sanctuary. The huge, colourful scene, ministering to thousands of viewers over the years, depicted the moment when the apostle Peter, stepping out on the stormy Sea of Galilee, took his eyes off Jesus and began to sink. Peter's arms are stretched out to receive the waiting, supportive hands of Jesus (Matt: 14:22-33). The artist, Bruce Erikson, later became an activist in the Downtown Eastside Residents Association and served as a Vancouver City Councillor for many years.

The big day arrived - Oct. 13, 1956. The dedication ceremony of the renovated Harbour Light Building was presided over by several dignitaries: Salvation Army Commissioner Edgar J. Dibden, International Chief of Staff from London, England, assisted by the Canadian Territorial Commander, Commissioner Wycliffe Booth (grandson of William Booth, founder of The Salvation Army) and British Columbia's Lieut. Governor, the honorable Frank M. Ross. The building was as impressive as the dignitaries gathered that day. The 200-seat chapel no longer needed to serve as the all-purpose room; a large dining area, a commercial kitchen, a recreation room with pool tables and shuffleboard, and a smaller 'coffee area' had been built in. A counselling room, immediately adjacent to the chapel, was also used as a free medical clinic hosted one evening a week by medical personnel. Added was a six-bed dormitory for men recovering from delirium tremens (D.T's, a severe, life- threatening form of alcohol withdrawal), essential storage areas, washrooms and offices, all on the main floor. Two upper floors would eventually house over 40 men in single rooms, and provide accommodation and office space for residential staff.

On the home front, Bill and Mildred rounded out their family with the arrival of Timothy Robert Leslie on March 16, 1957.

Increasing staff numbers were now essential to adequately care for the ever-escalating numbers of men seeking help on the road to recovery. Many of the graduates of the program were being employed, and/or volunteering for tasks in the Harbour Light Centre, positions ranging from assistant cooks, to cleaning, security, maintenance and clerical duties. The 'front desk' of Harbour Light, entry to the living quarters, was usually manned by a former client assigned to open (or keep firmly closed in the event of drunken confrontation) the door, to fellows like his former self, men seeking to escape the horrible streets.

Professional help was added with Salvation Army Officers being appointed as Assistants and, with a growing budget, a full-time bookkeeper. The answer-to-prayer financial genius was Major Hilda Hansen. Hilda was to become a much-loved legend for her compassionate care for her "lads" on Skid Row. The Hansen's, Lawrence and Hilda, were Salvation Army Officers in the Canada West Territory. Lawrence, plagued with rheumatoid arthritis and forced to apply for both leave from full-time Officership and a medical pension due to his deteriorating condition, was able to share Hilda's inherited family home in East Vancouver. Hilda and Lawrence both volunteered at the Harbour Light; Hilda more- than-capably managed the financial books while Lawrence carefully and prayerfully instructed converts to build their new way of living in Christ through the study of Biblical principles. He was promoted to Glory in 1962.

Since the Harbour Light opening, all costs had skyrocketed. 400 men were being fed each day and the costs of providing a full rehabilitation program were quickly multiplying. Major Hansen, clutching a fistful of bills, made her way to the 'Skipper's' office one busy day. Bill had been dubbed that affectionate title by the men on the program. Entering his office Hansen came to a full stop as she observed, spread out in full on the Skipper's desk, a set of blueprints "Captain!" she exclaimed, "What are we going to do? All these year-end bills are in my hand, and we have no money to pay *them*, never mind an expansion."

"Pray!" That was his answer. It was always his answer. Captain and Major were about to get down on their knees to address the all-knowing, almighty God right there on the floor of the office when the telephone rang. Bill reached over his desk to answer and listened closely to the caller's voice. "Captain Leslie," the female voice announced, "I was going to come over to Vancouver next week to bring you a cheque, but the Lord has laid it on my heart to send this gift in the morning mail." The promised letter arrived from Victoria the following afternoon containing five $1,000 savings bonds! The end of 1957 saw all bills paid plus a down payment on the small building right next door, 121 East Cordova. That expansion, opened in April, 1958, made way for an additional dining room for the men on the residential rehabilitation program, a realignment of service areas at the 119 address, plus a loading dock and storage.

There was another building, a large, usually empty, grungy garage, once again right next door to that newest purchase. Leslie would walk by and, when the owner wasn't around, pace all around the inside to pray and envision what God could do with that enormous space at 123 E. Cordova Street.

For two years he dreamed and prayed, but over that period of time he never felt assured that his plans were God's plans. It was until a night in early June 1960, when Bill heard a voice as clearly as though

someone was speaking directly in his ear: "Go ahead
and make that proposal to Headquarters." Leslie had his office
administrator type up a letter to the British Columbia Divisional
Commander, Brigadier Carl Hiltz, outlining his vision and noting
the property price of $60,000. It was two days later before a
phone call was received from Brigadier Hiltz.
"I got your letter, Bill, but what do you think has just happened?"
Hiltz asked.
"I don't know," Bill responded with a query in his tone. Excitement
bubbling in his voice Hiltz announced; "The current Property
Secretary in Toronto is being farewelled and I have been appointed
to take his place!" God's perfect timing again! The very man who had
national authority to approve or decline a property proposal was now
the man who knew every detail of Harbour Light progress. Within ten
days the proposal was sanctioned by Territorial Headquarters - with
the proviso that no monies for the property purchase would be
forthcoming from Territorial Headquarters.

In discussion with bookkeeper Hansen, Leslie learned that there
were sufficient funds on hand for a down payment on the property.
With the real estate sale papers in hand, Bill and Hilda walked up to the nearby

Canadian Imperial Bank at Main and Pender Streets to obtain a demand loan for $55,000.

The miracle on Cordova continued. As the Harbour Lighters prayed and trusted in God, money flowed in. One dollar and two dollar donations were lovingly offered by old-age pensioners, cheques arrived in the mail, service clubs responded with special fund-raisers and, in six months' time, the loan was paid off in its entirety! Renovations were completed by November providing a 500 seat chapel, a new, larger dining area, a craft room and plenty of storage. As a person entered the new chapel from the street they couldn't help but read the words 'MY GOD SHALL SUPPLY ALL YOUR NEEDS' at the front of the hall and, for thousands, in the years to come, those needs would be met.

Bill Leslie, a very complex man with a very simple faith, and a grade-8 education, became a sought-after expert in the treatment of alcoholism. He poured over medical journals and attended university seminars to garner the latest discoveries in addiction studies. He had no studies in psychology, but he knew the mind of the man on the street; he knew how to reach out and to lovingly draw that man to meet the One who could change his life - Jesus Christ. Bill excelled in the art of communication.

An informative newsletter, 'The Harbour Lighter' was being mailed out monthly, commencing in November, 1954. The simple 4-page document related the stories of lives dramatically changed, exciting answers to prayer, and the latest news of all the happenings at Harbour Light. In 1962, a 25-minute radio program was initiated on station KARI each Sunday afternoon and soon other radio stations in Penticton, Nelson, and Cranbrook signed on to air the simple programs. Bill, booming out the chorus of "*Throw out the lifeline*", began each broadcast and a loyal band of listeners eagerly awaited each week to hear from the musical 'combo' made up of current and former residents, testimonies from the converts, stories of God's provision, and a short devotional from "Banjo Bill". Those avid listeners and readers became generous supporters throughout the years.

Some listeners just became curious about what was happening in the notorious downtown area of Vancouver's Skid Row. They came to see what was happening and many got saved. One of those men was Jimmy Bryce, an immigrant from Scotland whonever lost his strong, colourful brogue. Jimmy wasn't a drunk; he had a permanent job with the Vancouver School Board, a lovely wife and two daughters. He showed up at an evening service at Harbour Light, was deeply convicted by the Holy Spirit and that evening gave his life to Christ. Jimmy later became a Sergeant of the Harbour Light Corps and he and his family were some of the most faithful proponents of the ongoing ministries.

Captain Leslie was in demand as a speaker, comfortable in any setting whether it be small groups or crowds of thousands such as a Salvation Army Congress meeting. He had a saying about public speaking: "Speaking is like drilling for oil; if you can't strike oil in 20 minutes, you're simply boring." The meetings that he led at the Harbour Light followed an easy formula: lots of rousing singing, testimonies from recent converts, a special music item, a brief sermon and an altar call. The sermon itself usually contained a joke, a story about how God had answered prayer or changed a life, along with a pointed message from the Bible. All of this happened within the 20 minute timeframe. What people who were seated facing the platform couldn't see was the text painted on the truss overarching the first row of seats in the chapel, John 12:21, "Sirs, we would see Jesus." The words were a constant reminder to whoever was occupying the platform that Jesus was to be presented first and foremost.

Bill helped produce a documentary movie, 'The Unknown City', telling the story of the Vancouver Harbour Light ministry in 1961. Though Bill did most of the filming and story outline, the material was edited and narrated by then Brigadier Arnold Brown, who was, in 1977, to become the Army's 11th General.

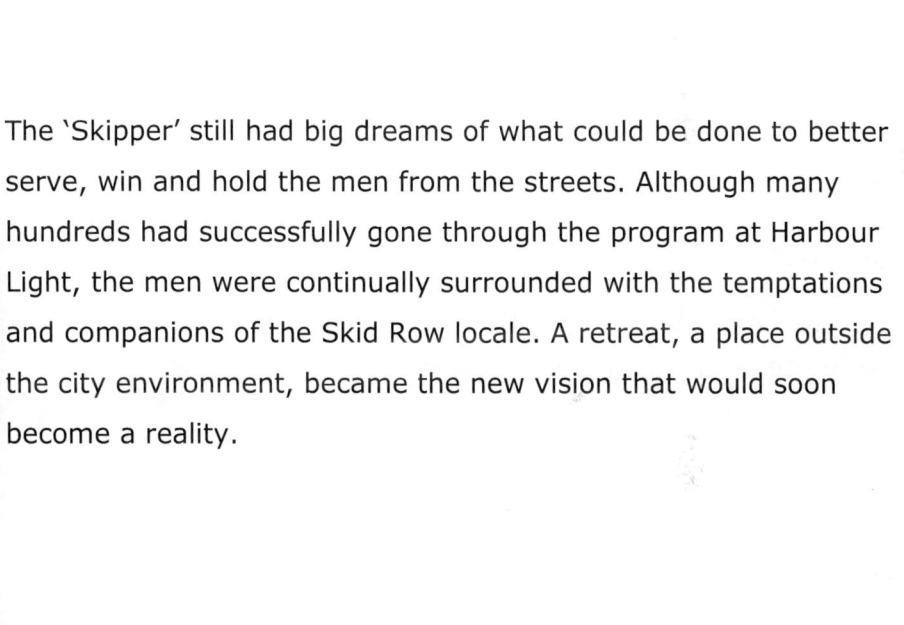

The 'Skipper' still had big dreams of what could be done to better serve, win and hold the men from the streets. Although many hundreds had successfully gone through the program at Harbour Light, the men were continually surrounded with the temptations and companions of the Skid Row locale. A retreat, a place outside the city environment, became the new vision that would soon become a reality.

Chapter 9 - Miracles of Grace

Lives dramatically and forever changed through the ministry of Harbour Light? It would take volumes of written work to record them all. Following are just a few examples of those miracles of love and grace:

Claude Crowell - the first convert - 1953. It was the first official meeting of the newly designated Harbour Light Corps, still operating out of that old, rat-infested smoke shop at 55A Powell Street, and it was Sept.16th when a highly inebriated Claude stumbled to the front of the crowded, smelly hall to receive Christ as his Saviour. A vibrant transformation took place in that moment. Who could have foretold that eventually Claude would become a valued employee of Vancouver's Salvation Army Grace Hospital?

Sid Bourne - Just before the new building at 56 Powell Street was opened, Bill Leslie received a call from local government health authorities asking if the 'Sally Ann' could help out an old man, sick and helpless in his skid row hotel room. "At that time," said Leslie, "we were in the midst of noisy, dusty renovations, but we fixed up a place for the old gent on the upper floor and put him to bed." Sid was the product of an elite background; his brother had

A Salvation Army Mercy Seat

been knighted by King George VI during W.W. II. His wealthy family, part of the English aristocracy of Montreal, had spent a fortune trying to ease Sid away from his addictions. That evening, sick, and feeling the gruesome effects of his latest alcoholic binge, Sid, drawn by the vibrant singing from the chapel, managed to grope his way down a long flight of steep stairs to listen to the music. On hearing the message and the invitation he, in spite of his befuddled brain, responded to the prompting of the Holy Spirit in his heart to accept Jesus as his Saviour. "Sid was sixty years old when we picked him up in that flophouse," recounted Leslie, "but after his conversion to Jesus he became one of the saintliest men I have ever met." On May 5, 1962, Sid Bourne passed on to his eternal reward. That incorrigible alcoholic had become a counsellor and Bible instructor to hundreds of men since the day of his salvation. What a funeral! 500 men jammed into the chapel while 300 more stood outside in the rain on Cordova Street - all patiently waiting to pass by Sid's open coffin. As they shuffled slowly by, some reached out to touch the coffin; others touched his hand, while each vet gave a respectful salute. All from the actual representation of a miracle of grace!

Ernie Welch - Ernie was a successful businessman in Penticton, B.C. before booze got the best of him. He was reduced to sleeping in the woods of Vancouver's Stanley Park in 1953. Daytime hours found him pan-handling on the streets, begging for anything that could get him another drink. It was a cold, wet, miserable October evening in when he lumbered his tall body into the Harbour Light chapel. Ernie got more than a meal that evening - he got to meet his Saviour. It was the words of the song by Stuart Hamblen,
'It is No Secret What God Can Do' that the Holy Spirit used to draw Ernie into a saving relationship with Jesus. Ernie progressed in his new life as a Christian to become an Envoy (a Salvation Army non-commissioned Officer) and eventually, the leader of the Harbour Light in Victoria, B.C.

Perly McCloud - a rough Scottish seaman, found a port he could not leave in Vancouver, B.C. The chains of addiction held him fast to the darkest streets of that harbour city. He frequented the Harbour Light for meals each night. One day, considerably inebriated, he knocked on Captain Leslie's office door and slurred, "Skipper, will you pray for me so that I will be able to keep out of the beer joints and get back to the meeting tonight and be saved?" That prayer was offered, and answered. McCloud did return that evening and got gloriously saved. He broke free from the chains of alcoholism that enslaved him, became a Master Mariner working on government ships based out of Victoria, B.C., and found his greatest pride was in being appointed the Corps Sergeant-Major at the Victoria Harbour Light Corps.

Endless names! Bill Kraft, Glen Boise, Eddie McLean, Bert Hodgson, Frank Mahoney, Bill Cruikshank, Ted Lockheed, Bill Young, Tom Vickers, Dick Lyons, Jack Owens, Johnny Johnson, Glen Currie, Jim Morrison, Cliff Phipps, and their individual stories of dramatic life changes go on and on. In the first 10 years of Vancouver Harbour Light ministry over 1600 folks were recorded as having claimed Christ as their Saviour and found new life at Harbour Light. *It is no secret what God can do*!

Chapter 10 – Miracle Valley

60 miles east of 119 E. Cordova Street, and a few miles North East of the city of Mission, B.C., at the remote end of the winding Stave Lake Road, stood a quarter section (160 acres) of spectacular second-growth forest. The only developed part of that acreage was a home built by a retired logger for himself and his wife on the southwest corner of the property, right beside the roadway. Changes in health were forcing the man to sell his retirement investment in the forested land. Bill Leslie and his Assistant Officer, Ron Poole, drove out to the site in late November, 1962. They had been praying and looking for some place that would become a sanctuary, a place of healing and restoration away from the busyness and seductions of the Vancouver asphalt jungle. Here, they firmly believed, was the answer to their prayers. They talked to the landowner and negotiated a sale - $14,500 for the property excepting the 10,000 square feet on which the house was built. The Salvation Army would have first right of purchase, at assessed value, when the owner decided to sell. To seal the deal the owner wanted 10% down, right now! Acting once again on faith, Bill and Ron determined that between the two of them they had enough in their personal bank accounts to cover the deposit. The

deal was done! They had just committed the Salvation Army to purchase and develop a piece of wilderness without a proposal or permission from Headquarters.

The necessary approvals and permissions arrived within six months to shore up the work already begun. Initially, a tent was pitched at the entrance to the site where the previous owner had cleared an acre of the forest. Within a week, a tar paper shack was erected to sleep 10 men and provide a crude kitchen with a wood stove for cooking and heating. Meanwhile, Ted, a Harbour Light graduate, now the centre's Public Relations Officer, came into his own. Ted Lockheed had more nerve than a toothache; he had no fear of approaching any businessman or woman in Vancouver and asking for help for this new arm of the Harbour Light, an arm which the men on the street were calling 'Miracle Valley'. From Domtar came truckloads of drywall, Finning tractor donated a bulldozer, a property developer let volunteers demolish and recover materials from homes he was going to clear for a new apartment block. As Ted capably schmoozed and bargained with multitudes of business people, another Harbour Light convert, Bud Lerette, spent 10-12 hour days 'picking up answered prayer' in the Centre's way-too-small, one-ton panel truck. (At a later time, Bud took temporary 'charge' of Miracle

Valley, working closely with Dick Lyons, recovering alcoholic and former head comptroller of the Canadian National chain of hotels, both working under Bill Leslie, and each dwelling in apartments situated over the newly-constructed, indoor swimming pool.)

A bus was procured from the West Vancouver transit fleet and outfitted with a small feeding area at the front. The bus, parked each morning, Monday to Saturday, in front of the jail doors at the rear of the police station on Main Street, waited to welcome the poor fellows who had been picked up on drunk and vagrancy charges the night before. A warm cup of coffee was available to each man along with the offer of 'three squares and a pack of tobacco' for anyone who wanted to take a trip out to the 'Valley' for the day. Most could not work but it gave them a day of sobriety and a chance to be in nature to help clear their minds.

In the daily evening meetings at Harbour Light the Skipper would ask for volunteers to help out with the construction going on at Miracle Valley. A former contractor, Carl Kruger was one of the first volunteers and he proved to be a true God-send. Carl knew how to design and build exactly what Bill Leslie envisaged. In a short time he had drawn up plans for the first lodge that was to be built with a basement designed for holding services, counselling and business offices, a central two-storey section with reception and recreation areas on the first floor, and 2 staff apartments on the upper floor. Adjacent to that central core would be two wings for accommodation, with washrooms and living areas for 18 men, plus an infirmary. The completion of that building, aptly named 'Kruger Lodge', brought the official opening of Miracle Valley in November, 1963. As the needs for the Valley developed, the call for volunteers became more specific: the need was for carpenters, electricians, plumbers, drywallers, painters, even the need for a water diviner! As each of those needs was met, the willing volunteers gained back their self-respect and pride in long forgotten skills that they had thought would never be used again. Out of that forest arose facilities to accommodate up to 400 people, a large dining area, workshops, a chapel, outdoor swimming pool, and a recreation center, mostly built with volunteer labour utilizing donated supplies. There was one particularly unbelievable exciting example of miracle provision: somehow, word got through to the Canadian Military Corps of Engineers based in Chilliwack, B.C. that The Salvation Army had some work going on in isolated conditions, a task that the engineers could help with. In short order, a command came down for this project to be a worthwhile exercise for a highly qualified and specialized team; a complete sewage system to be designed and installed at Miracle Valley!

The narrow, provincial roadway leading to the edge of Miracle Valley property was paved. The 200 hundred or more feet to the entry arch of Miracle Valley was not, and was nothing more than a sea of mud through which all the guests present for the opening of yet another building, had to slog their way. The Provincial Highways Department's colourful minister, Phil Gaglardi, had been invited to commemorate and officially open the new, two-storey Mary Copp Lodge, which he did with dignified humour and aplomb in spite of the fact that he also muddied his shoes to reach the building. It was only a short period of time before the B.C. Highways department dispatched a crew to pave the muddy roadway. "We pray about everything," Leslie chuckled with a lopsided grin, "but sometimes we just feel the need to give the Lord a nudge."

Support for the construction of the Mary Copp Lodge, and the later-built, much larger Copp Lodge, were gifts from J.P. Copp of Copp's Shoes.

Since the Vancouver Harbour Light was the conduit through which men were admitted to Miracle Valley, and the basic source of food and product, the day came when Major Leslie received a call from the kitchen staff at Miracle Valley. "We have no potatoes, no rice, no carbohydrates to fill our hungry residents." Bill called yet another urgent Harbour Light prayer meeting. Soon the prayer room became so filled with the presence of God, one felt they could almost reach out and touch the very God they were trusting to provide. Less than five minutes into the prayer time, a phone call was received at the front desk and the recipient of the call crashed noisily into the small chapel excitedly yelling, "We have potatoes! We have potatoes!" A farmer from Abbotsford was offering potatoes free of charge. "Just come and get 'em," he had said. Bud, the picker-up of answered prayer, arrived within the hour at the country farm. "You came in *that!*" the farmer scoffed as he directed the 1-ton panel truck driver to the massive barn. A sea of potatoes spread across the barn floor and banked the walls up to the 20-foot high ceiling…. thousands of pounds. Potatoes were not an issue for a very long time!

Miracle Valley would prove not only to be a rehabilitation centre, but a community service providing swimming and recreational facilities to that rural area of Mission. It also offered retreat facilities for churches and other groups to use the 300-seat chapel, dining facilities and accommodations. For many years, each summer the Valley hosted a two-week-long Bible conference featuring, among others, such prominent personalities as Dr. Charles Rolls, Col. Wesley Bouterse, Dr. J. Edwin Orr, Major Ed Read, Dr. Leonard Ravenhill and Dr. Fred and Mrs. Zarfas, (Mrs. Zarfas was known as the 'Scottish Nightingale' for her singing). The conference asked for no registration fees; it was a faith venture, and each year saw all conference expenses met and a surplus raised for missionary endeavours.

For that first Conference, water availability was expected to be sparse, even in the British Columbia rain forest, with the many extra guests on the premises. The engineers warned it would be so. "When you brush your teeth," Leslie laughingly urged the Conference guests while gently strumming his banjo, "just turn the tap on and off - don't leave it running or you could end up with a mouthful of toothpaste." Water proved to be plentiful!

It was Leslie's dream that the Chapel, yet to be built, would be the focus of the Valley, to stand proudly in the centre of the Complex. One day he energetically led a small group of folk on a walk into the forest and, after looking around, twisting and turning back and forth, he stopped. "Right here," he stated. 'Right here will be the Chapel. Let's pray right now and thank God for making it happen." Did God make it happen? You bet He did. A large, beautifully-simple, wood-frame building stands humbly in the midst of giant evergreen trees, with expansive windows on all sides offering an open view of the rich surrounding greenery.

Over time, Miracle Valley boasted many fine buildings – mostly built with the volunteer labour of men who were proud to be part of something positive and worthwhile and big, even as their own lives were being built or rebuilt. "I built that!" men would state proudly, pointing to a particular project. The form of labour wasn't without outside criticism: in spite of the expected negatives, many men learned skills for the first time in their lives, taught by other men whose lives were also being transformed from the tragic sting of alcoholism and addiction. Leslie, very conscious of Jesus' admonition, "Woe to you when all men speak well of you….." (Luke 6:26 NKJV), chose rather to ignore the negatives and concentrate on the leading of God's Spirit in all things. Through it all, tons of windows and doors were generously donated by Walker Windows and Doors in Burnaby, B.C., and some buildings were designed and constructed, under the hand of God, according to the product donated!

Under a later Salvation Army administration, Miracle Valley was eventually detached from Vancouver Harbour Light, renamed the "Cordula and Gunter Paetzold Rehabilitation Centre' in light of a generous support donation, and given a revised focus that adjusted to the growing needs of thousands of men, young and old, addicted to hard street drugs.

As society's rehabilitation programming ideas evolved, Miracle Valley's purpose came to a close in 2010. In the 48 God-blessed years of the life of Miracle Valley, over 35,000 men would find the hope of new beginnings and thousands of others would see their faith renewed and blessed. One of those men was Thomas Reid, who came to the Valley in 1965, totally broken in body and spirit. A miraculous transformation occurred when he too asked Jesus to be his Saviour. In a few months he was employed full time and, in March, 1969, he married the former Emma Douglas. Severe illness took him suddenly in September, 1969. For Tom's 'Promotion to Glory', Emma wrote a simple poem that was used in Tom's funeral, held at his beloved Miracle Valley. . .

Green Pastures: Still Waters

Just out of Mission City, tucked away between the hills, Lies a peaceful, quiet Valley
Where the soul for Jesus thrills. There, a pleasant habitation
For the seeker has been wrought Where a closer walk with Jesus Is the lesson daily taught.
Now a whole new Way is offered Men, with lives filled with strife
Finding help, and hope and healing and, in Christ, Eternal Life.

Chapter 11 – The Last Brigadier

If the first 10 years of the Harbour Light work were busy, the following years were gruelling. The expansion of Harbour Light work was not only the Vancouver buildings or the huge satellite work at Miracle Valley, but new ventures were being established throughout Western Canada. The 1960's saw Harbour Light Corps opened in Victoria, Prince George and Prince Rupert, then Red Deer and Calgary in Alberta and Winnipeg in Manitoba. Each of these ministries were initially manned and led by converts and previous Assistant Officers from the Vancouver site. Bill Leslie also took note of the changing street population.

The citizens were no longer the shell-shocked veterans from W.W. II or the Korean War. A younger crowd was emerging with emphasis on drug addicts, and folks with dual disorders (mental health plus addiction issues) were flooding the streets. Most street ministries were finding themselves to be in a growth industry.

Another demographic was noticeable as well, First Nations people. If there was ever a group that needed to be ministered to in a culturally sensitive way, it was many of these dear souls who found themselves ghettoized in the asphalt jungle of Vancouver.

In light of that need, Major Leslie went looking for more property. The location was to be in Northern B.C., a former ranch near Hazelton in the Kispiox valley, bordered by the Kispiox River, home of the world's largest steelhead. The land was purchased (*with* permission of headquarters) in late fall, 1970, but construction work would be hampered by severe winter weather conditions. The name of this project was to be 'Miracle Valley Ranch', and was to be designed for First Nations clients. Bud Lerette of Harbour Light pick-up truck fame became the on-site facilitator of the remote ranch program for its first year of construction.

The demands of expanded ministries and operational changes appeared to be handled with ease by Bill Leslie. In order to meet growing financial needs he spent more time speaking to community groups. One of the prominent members of a service club in Vancouver was heard to jovially remark, "Watch out for that Leslie, he gets your body acting up. You'll be holding a handkerchief to your eyes while you're reaching for your wallet." Bill was also in demand by the Salvation Army to conduct evangelistic campaigns and to speak to large Congress gatherings.

There were always musicians to be found among the converts of

Harbour Light. Leslie formed some into a 'combo'; a small group made up of a keyboardist or accordion player, a guitarist, a solo instrumentalist, and a bass player. Those few men could easily fit into a station wagon and hit the road whenever required. Some of those musicians were:

Vic Ricci – a cabaret singer with a magnificently deep, rich voice, was a smaller version of Dean Martin and a virtuoso on the accordion. He had a gift for being able to pull the singing voice out of most anybody he played for.

Johnny Johnson - a well-known band leader and former star junior football player in Vancouver, Johnny enthralled audiences with his skills on the xylophone, and he became the 'star' in the movie, *Out of The Shadows.*

Earl Ryan – a First Nation's Elvis, Earl was always a crowd favourite with his golden voice, guitar stylings and ready smile. Earl often referred to himself as an FBI, and then would laugh as he joked, "Full Blooded Indian."

Bert Hodgson - Bert began his music career in the North-Eastern

U.S. He started out playing the organ in movie theaters to accompany the silent movies of the day. He went on to enjoy the role of music director in many large churches throughout the U.S.A. Stan Sitar - a master accordionist who was, in his own words, "as happy as a curl on a pig's tail".

Each of these men had a world of potential in the music arena yet all of them had been thrown to the gutters by their addictions.
God performed a miracle in each of their lives and all were able to regain their talents, this time to glorify God.

There were also many musicians from the Salvation Army Corps and various churches in the Vancouver area that meaningfully connected with the Harbour Light and Miracle Valley ministries. Folks like the Keene family; 'Hap' Keene and his sons were gifted artists and frequent helpers at Gospel services. One son, Tom, went on to a music career with Youth for Christ and later became an accompanist/arranger for many notable Christian performers. Almost every evening a variety of groups and talented individuals would make themselves available to share Jesus in music.

In 1965, Captains Bill and Mildred were promoted to the rank of Major. Along with that promotion word was received that they were appointed as delegates to the Salvation Army's London, England, Centennial Congress. Bill was asked to be a speaker at the international gathering, to tell the Army world what God was doing through the ministries of Harbour Light and Miracle Valley. It was a warm and muggy night in July, 1965 when Major William Leslie was introduced to the crowd of thousands at Royal Albert Hall. In the ten minutes allotted to him, he powerfully told the stories of lives dramatically changed through the ministries in Vancouver and Mission. The most proud lady in the crowd that night was not Bill's wife, Mildred, but the lady seated beside her, Bill's mother, Ruth Leslie. She had last been in the Royal Albert Hall as a youngster, to hear the founder of the Salvation Army, William Booth, address the massive crowd. Tears of pride and deep gratitude flowed freely as an offering to the Lord for answered prayers for the salvation of her son.

Honours abounded to the reluctant Leslie. The National Film Board of Canada produced a documentary about the life of Johnny Johnson, one of the earliest converts, entitled "Out of the Shadows." In 1968,

Bill received another honour: Ray Sherwood, a contractor and proud member of the Lions Club in Vancouver, had his daughter submit an essay about the ministry of Harbour Light for the Lions Club International to choose a candidate for its 'Humanitarian of the World' award. Out of over 13,000 nominations received submission was chosen as the winner.

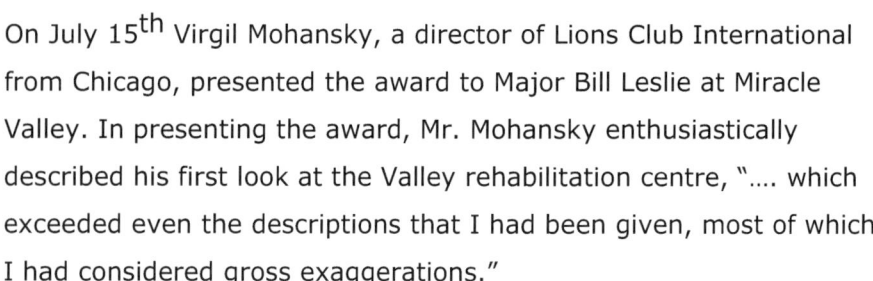

On July 15th Virgil Mohansky, a director of Lions Club International from Chicago, presented the award to Major Bill Leslie at Miracle Valley. In presenting the award, Mr. Mohansky enthusiastically described his first look at the Valley rehabilitation centre, "…. which exceeded even the descriptions that I had been given, most of which I had considered gross exaggerations."

Another event of 1968 was a planned tour of the Holy Land, Israel. A full busload of pilgrims, most of them converts and their family members, enjoyed 12 days of overwhelming spiritual refreshment walking in the land where Jesus had walked. The tour was so successful, and demand so great, that a second tour was organized for September of the following year. Two busloads of eager participants signed up for the adventurous tour but the temptation of the submitted final deposits resulted in the tour company manager absconding with the total funds. Sadly, some misguided, potential-tour folk laid the blame, and the theft, at Bill's feet. He was devastated and it took months for Bill to get back to his old self. It was not a good way to welcome the decade of the '70's.

With the increased growth of Harbour Light ministries a new title was given to the Major; he became the Regional Director of Services for Alcoholics for the Salvation Army in British Columbia. A final building on Cordova Street was purchased in 1970.

Number 153 Cordova Street, a small building adjacent to the "garage" was to accommodate a small detoxification unit*. This space contained 6 beds, a small clinic and staffing offices for a 24-hour service to help men detox before starting on the program at either Harbour Light or Miracle Valley. The need for this type of therapy was proven when the building was expanded and renovated to form Canada's first free-standing medical detox, hosting 30 beds in 1972.

New approaches to the treatment of addictions were constantly explored and programs were initiated to meet the needs of clients and their families. As contacts with the community grew there was interest from relatives and friends of the men in recovery to provide spiritual support and social opportunities. It wasn't just men on the street, but now the converts' wives and girlfriends made Harbour Light their church home. The Home League, a women's group, was formed to minister to the needs of ladies. Bowling leagues, family retreats to Miracle Valley, and the expanding Sunday Holiness meeting with its standard, sit-down roast beef dinner that followed the service, all helped to form this new church community of Harbour Lighters.

The Harbour Light 'family' spread far and wide. One simple story features a former oil-tanker engineer who, on release from 25- years in jail, had landed in a long-term care facility in a neighbouring community. He was sick and depressed, had been for some time; medical records indicated that George was dying. The wife of a former Harbour Lighter, newly employed as Chaplain in that facility, when reviewing resident names immediately recognized a Harbour

Light name. George had taken almost affectionate care of the obstinate heating equipment at Harbour Light during his residency there. Receiving no response from the large man curled into a ball on his bed, the Chaplain slipped an audio tape of Banjo Bill singing old Gospel favourites, into George's tape deck, left it playing, and did not return until the following day. Excited to be relinked with his Harbour Light family, George revived, relished regular Chaplain visits over the next three years, renewed his faltering faith in Christ, and died a contented man at age 91.

One of the vital anchors of the Harbour Light community was Brigadier Hilda Hansen, a widow, retired from active Salvation Army service in May, 1970. A faithful, prayerful volunteer, Hilda and daughter Eva continued to support the activities of the Harbour Light for the rest of their lives. Her office activities were later ably taken over by Brigadier Mildred Battrick.

The remote Miracle Valley Ranch in Kispiox, was proving to be one of the toughest challenges that Leslie had encountered. The land was purchased early 1970, but obtaining funds to build a new main lodge and renovate the existing structure, was becoming difficult. That first winter the few men in residence draped old sleeping bags along the walls to help keep out the bitter cold and frost. (The temperature plummeted to -60F on Christmas Eve!) Over 1200 kilometers away, and 14 hours of driving from Vancouver, the logistics in getting manpower and materials to the site were unreasonably difficult: local contractors and suppliers had to be hired and paid for. Construction was not able to start until December. On a particularly tough-winter trip from Vancouver to the Ranch, Bill, personally escorting a new resident in his car, was followed by the old Harbour Light truck, chock full of expensive, donated lumber. The arduous, wind-blown, snowy journey, most latterly winding up several miles of muddy, unpaved, dark, mountain switchbacks, took nearly 23 hours of constant travel. On arrival, the exhausted Major refused to rest until the truck, driven by Harbour Lighter Arne Morberg, also arrived, so his 'boys' could also eat and rest.

After another particularly gruelling trip to oversee the work at Kispiox at the end of Feb. of 1971, Bill stopped off at Miracle Valley on his way back home to just rest and relax. He dove into the comforting indoor swimming pool in the recently completed recreation complex and drifted, unmoving, to the surface of the water. Lifeguard John Moore, Harbour Light convert and later Administrator of Vancouver Harbour Light, immediately entered the pool and helped revive the unconscious Leslie. Doctor Hawkes, the

Valley's resident medical officer, diagnosed a heart attack attributed to stress. Hawkes knew his patient well and did more than just suggest time off. After hospitalization, knowing Bill would not take the rest he needed, Hawkes handed over tickets for flights and lodging for 3 weeks of forced rest in Honolulu. Bill and Mildred discovered a paradise they loved, and they rested well.

Another significant happening in the life of the Leslies' that summer was their daughter Anne's marriage to John Whitmore. The blessed event occurred in the Salvation Army Temple Corps, with Capt. James McCready (convert of the Sherbourne Street Hostel) officiating and Major Leslie proudly escorting his eldest daughter down the aisle.

1972 brought an announcement from the International Headquarters of the Salvation Army; there was to be a realignment of ranks for Officers. The rank of Brigadier was to be phased out during the year but there was also an allowance for Territorial Commanders to award the rank of Brigadier (usually given after 35 years of service) to officers who were deemed worthy of a promotion for meritorious service. Majors Bill and Mildred Leslie were given this honour.

It was not with humble gratitude that Bill received his promotion. In fact, he exploded with anger and indignation that an institution could hand out such awards to a few favorites while others were ignored and the "real" work of the Salvation Army was underfunded. This outrage was an outward manifestation of little hidden things that had, upon reflection, been eating away at him for some time. Over the years the Skipper had been given mementos by grateful clients, most notably, native carvings from First-Nations people. These beautiful works of art were now being given away by Bill. He also gave away his prized Grundig reel-to-reel tape recorder on which he used to listen to favourite messages from Bible teachers and conference speakers. We understand now that these were signs of deep depression in preparation for a potential suicide attempt. Perhaps God used the offered and rejected promotion to bring to light the terrors of Bill's inner being. When he threatened to resign his Commission rather than accept a promotion, the Canadian Territorial Commander, Commissioner Clarence Wiseman, phoned Bill with a personal invitation for Bill and Mildred to meet with the Commissioner and his wife in their Toronto home; the meeting took place on February 21st. Bill had often voiced the mantra that it was "better to burn out than rust out", but, in reality, he was a hurting man.

The Commissioner listened attentively as concerns were expressed and asked Bill if there was any way he could prioritize his work and reassign some of his duties to other staff. The Skipper agreed to the sagacious counsel. On leaving the Wiseman's home, Mildred, having quietly requested a private word, told the Commissioner that Bill would never wear a Brigadier's trimmings on his uniform, but requested that the promotion not be rescinded either, in order that there not be any rumours or speculation about having a rank pulled away. The Leslie's returned to Vancouver and Bill made the best efforts he could to finalize two projects.

One of those projects was the opening of a new Harbour Light building in Prince George, and the other, the opening of the Medical Detox* facility in Vancouver. These gargantuan projects resulted in Leslie's full physical and mental breakdown and resulting hospitalization on February 28, 1972.

" Burnout is a much better understood subject today. Extremely helpful resources are found in the videos from crestleadership.ca.

To top it all, a local, questionable socialite had boasted to the Vancouver Sun's gossip columnist that she had a new trophy in her case of conquests, Bill Leslie. The wise and understanding newspaper editor withheld the story but he did put a call into his friend, the Public Relations Director for the Salvation Army. "Whether the story is true or not", he told Major Stan Armstrong, "you've got to get Leslie out of town." By March 4th arrangements were in place for Bill to go to Honolulu where he would begin a doctor-ordered six month's Leave of Absence. Mildred would stay in Vancouver until June to see their two youngest children through school and to welcome their first grandchild.

Commissioner Wiseman had initiated protocols for the U.S.A. Western Territory of the Salvation Army to accept the Canadian Leslie's as officers of that territory. This step would allow for medical and salary benefits as well as the ability for Bill to take on light duties when deemed appropriate. They were accepted as Majors in the Hawaii Division and Bill was to take time to rest and recover in Honolulu. It was only two months later that he began to participate in conducting some meetings at the Men's Social facility in that city. In mid-June he was asked to train and lead a youth evangelistic team for a 6 week, cross-islands outreach. In the midst of that outreach word was received that the Leslies' were appointed as Island Commanders for Salvation Army operations on the big island of Hawaii commencing August, 1972, with their headquarters in Hilo. Before the end of that month, the Leslies' resigned their Commissions as officers in the Salvation Army and had returned to Canada.

Section 4 - You can start over again

> You can start over
> again, You can
> start over again!
> God will forgive you,
> He'll cleanse every stain!
> You can start over again!
> -Bill Leslie

Editors comment:

"Among all the biblical heroes, only Daniel (and possibly Joseph and Joshua) makes it to holy writ without recorded lapses and failures." (Charles R. Swindoll, *Moses A Man of Selfless Dedication.* P.19) Bill Leslie was not unlike the rest of us. Even King David, the 'man after God's own heart' who screwed up royally, records "For He Himself knows our frame; He is mindful that we are but dust." (Psalm 103:14). Bill Leslie was but dust–and God used him mightily.

Chapter 12 – Geographical Cures

Bill Leslie was feeling more like his old self again while in Honolulu, May 1972. He was cleared by medical staff to resume light duties and did so by helping out with services at Salvation Army centres in Honolulu. At the Men's Social Services Centre he ran across an old acquaintance, Betty Johnstone, who was working as a counselor at the Men's Social Services Department. A recently divorced Salvation Army Officer, Betty and Bill had met three years previously while Bill was conducting an evangelistic campaign in Pasadena, California. As all-too-often often happens when two lonely people meet, boundaries were crossed: physical intimacy was not an issue, but an emotional dependence was forming.

Mildred arrived at the end of June and the family took up residence in a house in the suburbs of Honolulu. Barely settled in, Bill escorted a youth team on their island-hopping ministry. It was during this time that Mildred and Betty had a 'conversation'. They were quite opposite both in appearance and personality. Mildred, quiet and compassionate, was a loving and ever-supportive part of Bill's life. Her husband's breakdown had stiffened her resolve to keep the family strong and together. Betty, totally American, brassy and forthright, had scraped her way up from a life of poverty, and more latterly had been rejected by her husband for a younger woman. Betty was a statuesque blond while Mildred, a brunette, had a more petite frame. Needless to say, they were not compatible.

Mildred, sensitive as always to the work Bill was doing, wisely waited until he was finished with that responsibility before confronting him about their future together. Decision made; they would resign by giving notice to the appropriate Salvation Army personnel, leave Hawaii and return to Vancouver.

Back in B.C., Bill and Mildred took opportunity to enjoy being grandparents while staying with family and friends. Daughter Anne, and John, rarely had a chance to hold their own precious daughter, Jodi, because of the grandparental attention she received. However, there was now a strained atmosphere in the area they had known for the past 19 years.

The Leslies' had cut their ties with the Salvation Army, a step that not only had financial implications, but social costs as well. One could not know, unless they had served in the Army, what a pervasive influence and hold the Salvation Army culture had on a person. It was not cultish, but a way of life that fully embraced a person, similar to that experienced by persons in the R.C.M.P. or other forms of military organization. Friends and peers did not understand what could motivate such a drastic step that would cause them to leave The Salvation Army. Following several futile attempts to find meaningful work, Bill and Mildred agreed that a long-distance change was needed. They packed up their belongings and moved to Bill's home town, St. Mary's, Ontario.

In the town of approximately 7000, they found a refreshing new start. Their fellowship was with extended family and in reconnecting with old friends. Mildred renewed her Ontario Nursing accreditation and was soon working in the small St. Mary's hospital. Bill obtained employment as an addictions counselor for a medical clinic. The youngest children, Tim and Kathie, were enrolled at the local high school and the family was domiciled in a rented house. Bill found his job very fulfilling but a difficulty arose; men and women were being led to the Lord through Bill's work, but, as persons seeking to conquer addictions, they were unable to find accepting church homes (hauntingly like the situation faced by William Booth, founder of The Salvation Army, in the mid 1800's.) Leslie approached Divisional Headquarters in London, Ontario in November, 1972, with an idea. He proposed that he and Mildred manage the local Salvation Army Corps (currently operating without Corps Officers) as lay leaders, in exchange for housing. They would continue to work in their respective occupations, while co-ordinating Corps programs and providing a discipling ministry for new believers. The response was less than positive. "You're an embarrassment to The Salvation Army," * the unforgiving Divisional Commander sarcastically told Bill as he rudely rebuffed their offer. With that curt, dashed hope of a future, Bill reverted back to floundering in depression; old wounds were rubbed raw with overwhelming feelings of failure in all areas of his life. Bill Leslie became a different man.

That sentiment was not shared by more senior Salvation Army leadership. Commissioner Wiseman, who later became 'General' of The Salvation Army, often reached out to the Leslie's with genuine offers of caring help.

It was October 6, 1973, when the Leslie's oldest son, Paul, married Joy Christie in Port Alberni, B.C. It was a good and positive occasion as the Christie and Leslie families joyously celebrated together.

"Your father and I are separating." Paul received the tearful phone call just a week after the wedding. Mildred explained that the previous eleven months had seen their marriage breaking apart, strand by strand, and that Betty was in the middle. Since Paul had been commissioned as a Salvation Army Officer just a year before, Mildred and Bill had mutually agreed it was best to keep their personal situation under wraps so as not to disturb Paul's fledgling ministry. The situation had now changed: in order to marry Joy, Paul had had to resign from Officership, as, according to regulations at that time, Officers could marry only Officers.

Bill was now sharing a dwelling with Betty and both were involved with youth work in a program called Fernie House in Pickering, Ontario. Interestingly, the motto of Fernie House was at the opposite end of the spectrum from the work to which Bill had so passionately sacrificed himself for all those years: *It's better to build strong youth than repair broken men.*

Chapter 13 – Fernie House

George Fernie, walking home on a cold, wintery Sunday from Danforth Street's Presbyterian Church in Toronto, happened upon a scared young boy, shivering, alone, and hunched in a storefront. George took the homeless, hungry 16-year old to a coffee shop and listened as the lad, just released from 14 days in jail for petty theft, poured out his story of neglect and abuse. That day George vowed he would do something to help kids in similar circumstances. Through practical service and lobbying with denominational officials, a suitable building on a large property was purchased in Pickering, Ont. In 1972 Fernie House* was opened as a place of refuge for the rebuilding of young lives. It was a ministry of the Presbyterian Church in Canada in co-operation with Durham County Children's Aid Society. Fernie House would shelter up to 18 boys. Sadly, later NIMBYism saw that number drop to 10.

Bill and Betty were hired as a team to provide administration, public relations and counseling services for the residents. Many of the children came from homes where addictions were rampant and most from backgrounds of poverty. Betty, having also grown up in poverty, clearly identified with their childhood experiences: her family had been constantly on the move while earning a living from harvesting in the orchards and farms of California. With taunts and jeers of 'white trash' still echoing in her mind, Betty readily empathized with the tragic life stories of the young residents. Bill and Betty figured the most affordable way for the two of them to live in the expensive Metropolitan Toronto area would be to purchase a motorhome and park it at their workplace: the motorhome proved to be key to success during their eight-year engagement at Fernie House.

Bill's responsibilities included fundraising and counselling. As the children awakened to the love that brought genuine improvement in their situations, some became open to committing their lives to Christ, and did so. Betty, an accomplished keyboardist, and Bill with his banjo, took young Christians to churches in and around Toronto for the children to share their testimonies and for Bill to speak about the ministry of Fernie House. Using tried and true techniques, regular newsletters were sent out to encourage the supporters whose generous giving sustained the outreach program. Soon invitations to speak were being generated from outside the Greater Toronto Area, and the good travel weather of the summer months provided opportunity for Fernie House to become known nationally throughout the Presbyterian Church. An excited caravan of folk would set forth from Pickering with the motorhome towing a large trailer followed by vans with kids and staff members; east to the Maritimes one year, west to British Columbia the next.

On Oct. 20, 1974, Paul and Joy welcomed a baby daughter, Kari, into their lives. Paul was now stationed as Assisting Officer at the Sherbourne Street Hostel while Joy studied as a 'cadet', in the Salvation Army Officer Training College in Toronto. The bliss, and sleeplessness, of experiencing a newborn was interrupted for a few days when Paul travelled out of town with his mom, Mildred, to offer support during divorce court proceedings. In the days of 'no-fault' divorce, one can barely imagine the gut-wrenching awfulness of hearing one's own father, or husband, publicly confessing to living in an illicit relationship. Nor could one forget the sound of the judge's commanding gavel, three times striking the gavel base, each ear-splitting blow offering a plea from the Court for reconciliation. The last blow ended with an ominous silence; then came the pronouncement - Decree Nisi granted. Decree Absolute was signed and declared on Jan. 27, 1975. Bill and Betty were married on Feb. 4, 1975.

The decade of the 1970's was chock full of mixed emotions and experiences: additional grandchildren, the marriage of youngest daughter, Kathie, to Dale Alary, school graduations, Mildred returning to Officership (July, 1977), Bill's infrequent letters filled with Scripture, increasingly fewer calls from Bill to his children, and only a couple of brief visits to see grandchildren. In 1981, Bill and Betty chose to end their employment at Fernie House. Bill's health was faltering; deteriorating eyesight and heart issues, both from Type-2 diabetes, were taking a toll.

The couple bought a bigger motorhome and went to do what Bill loved, living by faith and preaching the Gospel.

**Fernie House has become a major resource for services to youth. Go to their website at fernieyouth.ca.*

Chapter 14 - Missions and Miracles

Living the R.V. lifestyle totally suited Bill and Betty who primarily followed the sun, criss-crossing the U.S.A. Eventually they had two 'home' parks, one close to Houston, Texas and the other in Tampa, Florida. In early fall they made a point of visiting Bill's relatives and seeing specialists for his medical care. While in Ontario they were based at Bill's sister's apple orchard, near London. Helen and Jerry would have their harvest in, and the storage area cleared out for bales-of-hay seating to accommodate the week-long Gospel sings that would be packed out with relatives, friends and neighbours. Bill consistently shared exhilarating new stories of lives transformed and of God's miraculous supply.

Bill had a new sense of calling now. Not being as pressured and frenetic as in the past, he had time to reflect upon God's grace in restoring his faith and giving him a new field of ministry. It had taken years for Bill to forgive himself, to acknowledge that God had never forsaken him, and to become more aware of God's everlasting love surrounding and blessing His child. Bill had to live with the consequences of his decisions, as we all do. He learned that it's not just a verse in the Bible, but a true reality that "He (God) is the same yesterday, today and forever." (Heb.13:8)

Periodically the motorhome would find its way over to the West Coast to Portland, Oregon, where Betty would visit with her children, then Bill would hop up to Vancouver to get reacquainted with old friends and take opportunity to hold his grandchildren.

For eight to nine months of the year, Bill and Betty would be invited to hold weekend or week-long evangelistic services in various churches. An old friend, Colonel Bram Tillsley (later promoted to being the 14th General of the Salvation Army), had become the Territorial Commander for the U.S. Southern Territory in 1985. He offered the Leslie's an option to become contract Territorial Evangelists for the territory's Adult Rehabilitation Centers (ARC). This, a link back to minister in environments they both knew so well, was an offer they could not refuse.

The pattern of starting out from one of their home bases to do a series of four to five nights of meetings and a few days of counselling at assigned rehabilitation centres, yielded results; dozens of folks got right with God each week. Bill was invited to do an evangelistic campaign in Haiti for the Salvation Army. To work internationally was a new experience, especially since his French language skills were limited to a few basic words like 'Chevrolet Coupe', which he would pronounce 'coupay'. Bill fell in love with the Haitian people. On returning to the States he organized fresh water projects, encouraged each rehabilitation centre where he and Betty were ministering, to pledge to supply a truck load of piping, pumps, clothing and medical supplies to be transported to Miami. From there the desperately-needed items were loaded into shipping containers and sailed to Haiti, where they, under the supervision of Salvation Army personnel, were unloaded and distributed to needy villages.

Bill and Betty answered another missionary call, this time from the Caribbean Territory, to conduct meetings in Jamaica. Reunited with a Salvation Army colleague, Col. Ed Read, they were sent out to May Pen, a small community near Kingston. Because of the tremendous demand, the weekend's campaign kept being extended, culminating in two-weeks of revival meetings that resulted in the 'planting' of a new Salvation Army Corps (church).

Back in Canada, Tim, Bill's youngest son, was commissioned as a Salvation Army Officer in June, 1984, then married Lieutenant Miriam Crews on January 14th. Mildred had taken early retirement from the Salvation Army in 1982 and established residence in Surrey, B.C.

Chapter 15 – Final Promotion

1988 brought disheartening medical news for Bill. Ongoing heart problems necessitated open-heart surgery but the condition of his eyes was a complicating factor. Laser surgery was keeping sight deterioration at bay, but it was felt that the current techniques of heart surgery could cause loss of eyesight. Bill promised to watch his weight and to take part in light exercise, but he was not willing to risk his ability to see.

It was on the afternoon of Jan. 13, 1989 that the motorhome was made secure in the parking lot of the Salvation Army's Adult Rehabilitation Centre in New Orleans. The weather, with overcast skies, had been muggy and cool by Louisiana standards. Just a few blocks from the Centre the Meccano-like structure of the Huey Long Bridge was visible. Preparations were underway for the upcoming Mardi Gras celebrations, with hawkers already on the streets selling the gaudy hats and purple necklaces associated with that party time. Bill and Betty made their preparations for the upcoming services in the chapel of the rehab centre. The attendance was small that evening, but the reception was warm to the music and message that God had laid on Bill's heart. One young man walked forward to the

Mercy Seat that night. Bill prayed with him and made an appointment for next morning to help counsel him on first steps in walking with Jesus Christ.

It was next morning when Bill woke to a clearing sky and, following a walk around the blocks surrounding the rehab centre, he met the young convert who was waiting for him. Bill offered a Bible and useful handouts on how to study the Bible, and then listened to the man's life story of how he wound up on the streets of New Orleans. Bill encouraged this 'new creation' in Christ with stories of others who had walked similar paths and how their lives were changed, made new, and how God would now walk alongside him. A prayer of thanksgiving for what the Lord was now doing in this man's life followed and they agreed to meet again at that evening's service. Bill made his way to the motorhome where Betty had readied a lunch of hot soup. After the usual expression of thanks to God for the food, Bill lifted his spoon but before he could take that first mouthful, his face hit the bowl. He had suffered a massive brain-stem hemorrhage. Betty acted immediately and a screaming ambulance soon transported Bill to hospital. Calls were made to family members.

The following morning, son Tim left from Saskatchewan to travel to New Orleans. Paul and Kathie were awaiting their flight to depart from Vancouver when, as they were about to board, the ticket agent passed along a call just received; Bill had gone to be with the Lord just before noon from that hospital room in New Orleans. He never regained consciousness; he had experienced no pain in his final hours. On Jan. 15, 1989, at the age of 63, "Banjo" Bill Leslie had received his final promotion - "Promoted to Glory."

Paul continued on to New Orleans. Betty, Tim and Paul, made careful plans over the next few days for the best ways for Bill to be honored. Two services were arranged, one in his home town of St. Mary's, Ontario, another back at the Harbour Light in Vancouver. Paul, and Betty, attended the memorial service in the new Salvation Army Corps building in St. Mary's, Jan. 21, 1989, where Colonel Roy Calvert, the Field Secretary for the Salvation Army in Canada, led the service. Roy had campaigned with Bill in 1965 as part of the Centennial Cavalcade that went across Canada to celebrate the Army's 100th Anniversary. The service paid tribute to a life well-served. Family and friends were given opportunity to share their memories about Bill's life. Brigadier Vic Greenwood's words were especially descriptive of the young Lieutenant he had mentored so many years before. "He was like a young stallion. I just had to learn to hold the reigns lightly and let him run as he was called to do."

In Vancouver, Tim and Kathie worked with Harbour Light's Commanding Officer to coordinate a service planned for Jan. 27th, in the chapel of the new building: that building was opened in Oct. 1987, replacing the old structures on Cordova Street. The Commanding Officer was Capt. John Moore, the same Moore who was a convert of Harbour Light and who had saved Bill's life while serving as a lifeguard at Miracle Valley. Tributes were paid by Bill's friend, Commissioner Ed Read, and Claude Crowell (Harbour Light's first convert), and the City of Vancouver as represented by Alderman Don Bellamy. Many other friends and associates kept the celebration of the Skipper going for hours as the crowd lovingly continued to reminisce, using the large dining area.

Denny Boyd, a respected columnist with the Vancouver Sun newspaper, penned a colorful eulogy, parts of which read: "When Bill Leslie arrived in 1953 to bring salvation to Vancouver's Skid Roaders, whether they were asking for it or not, he wasn't packing the 'terrible swift sword' of divine retribution. He was armed with a stew pot and a banjo... Eighteen years ago, John Moore woke up among the garbage cans of East Cordova and Columbia, his last stop on a Canada-wide drunk, and, shaking with the chuck horrors, went to the old Harbour Light, where he met Bill Leslie, had some of his stew and some of his kindness. 'He gave me hope when there was nothing else,' says the man who followed Leslie into the Army. 'You thought of him as a bigger man than he was because he was so huge through the chest. He had piercing blue eyes, and what set of pipes he had. I can still hear him singing *The Old Ship of Zion*, and the rummies joining in on the chorus, *Ship Ahoy, Ship Ahoy*'... From a two-burner stove in a smoke shop, Leslie expanded Harbour Light into a centre that became a six- million dollar building with 24 detox beds and 32 residential rooms that opened last year... and Miracle Valley, 20 kilometers from Mission City, a long-term treatment centre was also Leslie's vision..."

On January 28th Mildred, along with her four children, their spouses and the grandchildren, quietly drove to Miracle Valley. It was quiet, peaceful, overcast and cold day with a dusting of snow on the ground. They drove through the grounds to the recreation centre, opened in 1969. It was the only building of either Miracle Valley or Harbour Light, to ever have the name 'Leslie'* attached to it. A small plaque over the shallow end of the indoor pool named it the 'Earl

Leslie Pool', in honor of Bill's dad, who had encouraged his son in athletic endeavors.

Climbing silently out of their vehicles, the sorrowing family quietly meandered down the narrow dirt path, lovingly-formed Meditation Trail. The Trail led to an outdoor prayer chapel where Miracle Valley residents had carved out log seating and constructed a simple, log cross. About half-way down the trail, at the foot of a group of small trees, the mourners collectively chose a spot for the earthly remains of Bill to rest. Tim and Paul dug a small hole where the ashes were buried then deliberately left it with no memorial stone or marking. For such a public figure, this was to be a place of solitude and tranquility. Each family member stood with tearful, silent memories. Paul offered a simple prayer of Committal. William Ronald Leslie's final resting place was in the forest of the valley of miracles.

*It *wasn't until Harbour Light's Golden Jubilee, November 9, 2002, that a Dedication Plaque, celebrating the ministry of Bill and Mildred Leslie, was placed at the 119 E. Cordova Street location. General Bram Tillsley with his wife, Maude officiated at this memorial event.*

EPILOGUE

The writing of each chapter of this book evoked a lot of memories and a lot of emotions. My father, as all good Dads should, shaped my life in so many ways. I loved him, wanted to be like him and, for the longest time, never felt I could measure up to him. My mother also helped to make me who am. I am Mildred in my love of reading, quiet contemplation, and addiction to watching sports (the alternative for those of us who cannot play the games). Like any other family we went through our ups and downs, times of great joy (our holidays at Montibello Court in Santa Cruz, California) and our times of regret and sorrow. I am thankful to say that, eventually, Bill and Mildred became friends again.

Mom went to be with her Lord just 23 months after Dad's passing. She was looking after her grandchildren on the evening of December 27, 1990, when she suffered a massive heart attack.
My wife, Joy, and I, were both working evening shifts at our respective jobs. (We had resigned as Officers the previous July.)[*]

[*] A document, found after Dad's death, helped solidify this decision. Dad had

requested a statement of what his pension would be from the Army, upon reaching the age of 65. After 27 years and 3 months of service he would be awarded $78.86 per month. In the mid 1990's, the Ontario government took the Army to court, to enforce pension reforms. The Supreme Court ruled in favour of the government and the pension situation for officers is much improved. The decision, however, was not 'grandfathered'.

Mom was rushed to the hospital where both Joy, and Mildred's daughter, Kathie, were working. The two loving nurses gently whispered comfort to her as she quietly slipped into the receptive arms of her loving Saviour. Despite wet, treacherously slippery snow, family, friends and fellow Officers packed the Vancouver Southmount Corps on December 31st to honour her life that New Year's Eve. She now rests in the section of graves reserved for Salvation Army Officers at Ocean View Memorial Park, Burnaby, B.C.

Betty faded out of our lives after Dad's funeral. She, and the motorhome, moved to Portland, Oregon. In 2020, word reached us that she had remarried before passing away.

Harbour Light continues an active ministry with the residents of Vancouver's Downtown Eastside. The address remains, but the building is entirely different. In 1986 the old structure was demolished to

make way for an impressive six- million dollar building opened in October of the following year. The 500-seat chapel was downsized to accommodate 125. The McCready residence's 44 individual apartments and a new medical detox unit are key components of the edifice. The mercy seat (prayer bench) is, sadly, no longer the primary source of entry to rehabilitation for the clients. Current culture emphasizes medical and social care to the detriment of a focus on spiritual care.

This was made strikingly clear to me when I attended the Street Level Conference in 2006, sponsored by the Evangelical Fellowship of Canada, where one of the keynote speakers was Commissioner Christine MacMillan**, The Salvation Army's Territorial Leader for Canada.

Having known Chris before she entered Officer's Training College in the '70's, I was comfortable approaching her after the plenary session and asked how things were going with the Vancouver Harbour Light.

"We have no one willing to take on the work in Vancouver," was her mind-numbing reply. "Would you take on the job?" Chris' question floored me. I was unable to accept her gracious offer, but it deeply saddened my heart. The Army, with its vast resources and personnel, could not locate one special someone who had a burning passion for those most wounded and lost.

History records so many, many predecessors who had willingly jumped at the opportunity to meet Christ's mandate to serve the least among us.

> ****I hope that one day, someone will publish a book about the women officers, like Christine, who have reached out with such love and compassion, who have proven the capability, and necessity, of women in ministry.**

Miracle Valley actively thrived for many years, but the dawn of a new century brought unhappy tidings. A full review of operations and facilities was ordered, to see how, or if, the Valley could adapt to 21st century culture. Advanced building codes, seismic requirements and changing government legislations meant a massive overhaul was needed. Many of the buildings were deemed too expensive to remediate in compliance with new standards. Decisions were eventually made to build new facilities to accommodate a maximum of 172 persons. Many of the old buildings were released to the city of Mission's Fire Department for live burning drills. The recreation centre and pool were bulldozed to eliminate the building's hazardous materials.

Construction produced new resident accommodations and a modern kitchen/dining/conference area named after Commissioner Leslie Pindred. Financial resources for the construction projects were largely donated by one family in return for naming rights. Miracle Valley became 'The Salvation Army Cordula and Gunter Paetzold Rehabilitation Centre'. In 2008 Major Robert Ratcliff was appointed as Executive Director and asked to work with Divisional Headquarters staff in determining the future viability of the centre. Declining numbers of clients being referred to the centre, and fewer grants and donations being made available, all spoke to the inevitable future that Miracle Valley's days as a rehabilitation centre were numbered.

In spite of declining resident numbers, Chaplain Dianne Holland, hired in 2008, joyfully recorded the names of many men over the next two years, who began their new lives in Jesus, life changes that often began from a broken man kneeling at the mercy seat seeking forgiveness and salvation, then nurtured by caring Miracle Valley counselling staff.

July 14th, 2010 was the day set aside by the Army for the demise of Miracle Valley. The event was intended to be a celebration of many years of success.

Like most funerals though, for many, the sense of sorrow was overwhelming. Three generations of Leslie's attended the event: Tim, and I, Paul, with my son Ryan, and toddler grandson, William Leslie, (nicknamed, Liam). Tim masterfully coaxed Gospel music from the old Chapel piano and voices in the over-filled building lifted in such a manner that the very high-beam rafters joined in songs of praise to the One who had dramatically changed the lives of thousands of men. I had been asked to give testimony to what Miracle Valley meant to me and, as I stood on the platform, feeling strangely akin to my father, Bill Leslie, my hand swept above and across the mercy seat with reference to the years of tears that had flooded that stained prayer bench.

The meeting closed with a final word from the Divisional Commander, Major Susan L. van Duinen, followed by a formal folding and laying to rest of The Salvation Army Miracle Valley flag. Best of all, as the last song crescendoed across the sunlit Valley, a young man walked firmly down the aisle and deliberately knelt at the Mercy Seat, offering his heart to Jesus. What could be a more fitting closure for a 48-year ministry that had blessed tens of thousands?

The Cordula and Gunther Rehabilitation Center, so fondly previously known as Miracle Valley, was listed for sale at $6,500,000 and was purchased by a Sikh group for an undisclosed price. The property now serves as a Sikh youth camp.

I have many great memories of my Dad. One of the most memorable is from the 1970 Miracle Valley Bible Conference. I found Dad in the Chapel one afternoon, polishing the Mercy Seat with a lemon-oil-soaked cloth. He looked me directly in the eyes: "This is the greatest joy in ministry", he genuinely smiled, "to polish away the tears of people kneeling here to find the Lord, and to pray for new souls that will cry here as well." It wasn't until years later, as the scarcity of that form of prayerful practice became the norm, that that memory became so precious.

Finally, one closing song, penned by Sidney Cox, number 335 in the 1987 Salvation Army Songbook, the chorus and third verse:

I want to tell you what the Lord has done, what the Lord has done for me;
He lifted me from the miry clay; O what a happy day!
I want to tell you what the Lord can do, What
the Lord can do for you;
He can take your life as He did mine
And make it anew.

What God has done, He still can do; His power can fashion lives anew,
And all who trust Him find Him true; Can you wonder that I want to tell it?

Appendix 1

An influence across the decades

Miracle Valley Graduation testimony - April 28, 2010 -Todd Shaw

"First of all I would like to thank the staff here at Miracle Valley for their patience, hard work, compassion and understanding. You are all very special people, not unlike surgeons and fire fighters; you all save lives - including mine. I say that from the whole of my heart.

"Miracle Valley was founded by Bill Leslie in the 1960's. Bill fundraised and used the labour of skid row alcoholics to build the original buildings including this chapel. Bill had an idea that you could take an alcoholic, if he wants help, to a safe place to detox and then spend 3-6 months learning about the 12 steps, God, and themselves. They could heal and change their lives...

"...God called upon Bill and Betty to take over and direct 3 large group homes in Ontario owned by the Presbyterian Church, called Fernie House. In 1976 I was placed there by the Children's Aid Society. I had been in 18 different homes by age 12, physically and sexually abused, abandoned by my family who had moved to

Alberta. I was angry, delinquent, violent and abusive. Until this time all male authority figures had beat and abused me. "Banjo" Bill Leslie never touched me, or even yelled at me. He even liked me, told me so, gave me special chores of which paid me cash….so I could save up and buy cool clothes. Bill took me fishing, to church, and to the Maritimes. I was also in the house choir; quite simply I loved Bill Leslie like a father and he always saved my butt when I was in trouble…

"…When I left Fernie House in 1978, Bill sat me down and said, 'Todd, if you ever have a problem with alcohol or drugs, go to Miracle Valley, they will help you; and tell them I sent you." Now, after 32 years, 17 in jail and 28 years of using, I found myself in the penitentiary doing five years, tired and broken…the Correctional Counselor seemed distant and hesitant until I played the Bill Leslie card. The fix was in. When I arrived here I was questioning the therapy, counseling and God stuff but I was on parole and not graduating would cost me another 2 years in jail. I began to work on my behavior, core beliefs and take direction and began to establish a new identity.

"You can close the Valley, and I can leave and move on, but you will never take away what Bill Leslie and the staff here has done for me. All the staff here will take Miracle Valley with them and share and spread the message of Jesus and recovery elsewhere. Thank you Jesus and Bill Leslie! "

Appendix 2

Officers who served at Harbour Light or Miracle Valley, 1952-1972

Commanding Officers and Assistant Officers

1952 - 1953 Sr. Major David (Rhoda) Hammond* assisted by C.S.M. George Hodson*

1953 - 1972 Captain William (Mildred) Leslie
1954 - Lieut. William Bird
1955 - Lieut. Arthur Kloepfer

1956 - 1958 Capt. &. Mrs. Archie MacCorquodale
1958 - Lieut. Hugh Thompson
1959 - Lieut. Ron Trickett

1960 - Capt. & Mrs. George Wright
1961 - 1963 Lieut. Ronald (Vera) Poole
1963 - Capt. Bill (Dorothy) Bird
1964 - Envoy & Mrs. Ernie Welsh

1966 - 1968 Capt. & Mrs. Jim McCready
1967 - Capt. & Mrs. Albert Ferris (M.V.)
1968 - Capt. & Mrs. Burt Dumerton
1968 - Capt. & Mrs. Morgan

(M.V.) 1969 - Capt. & Mrs. Bruce

Harcourt 1969 - Major & Mrs. Tom Bell

(M.V.) 1970 - Capt. & Mrs. Albert Ferris

1970 - Capt. & Mrs. William Ratcliffe

(M.V.) 1971 - 1975 Capt. & Mrs. William Head

1972 - Major & Mrs. Robert McKerracher (M.V.)

1972 - Col. John (Grace) Nelson

1972 - Capt. & Mrs. Albert Ferris 1972-76

Appendix 3

While serving as the Salvation Army's Public Relation Officer in Vancouver, I (Sam Fame) piloted the opening of the new Harbour Light on 119 East Cordova Street.

Never in my wildest imagination did it occur to me that in 1991, due to family circumstances, my wife and I would appointed to the Vancouver Harbour Light.

- two years as Assistants followed by thirteen years as Executive Directors. We were honored to follow in Bill Leslie's footsteps. Being mindful of the passion that drove him and the pitfalls Satan uses to undermine God's work, the life and work of the Leslies remained uppermost in my heart and mind. It was our dream and privilege to reach Harbour Light's 50th Anniversary to honour Majors 'Banjo Bill 'and Mildred Leslie with a Golden Jubilee Anniversary Plaque, giving honour where honour was due.

THE GOLDEN JUBILEE PLAQUE
DEDICATED IN HONOUR OF
MAJORS 'BANJO BILL' AND MILDRED LESLIE WHO OFFICIALLY OPENED

VANCOUVER HARBOUR LIGHT ON SEPTEMBER 15, 1953,

FOUNDED AND OPENED MIRACLE VALLEY ON NOVEMBER 22, 1963

AND PROVIDED DYNAMIC LEADERSHIP AND MINSTRY TOGETHER, WITH COMPASSION, FAITH AND PRAYER, UNBOUNDING ENERGY AND A LOVE FOR SOULS, THE LESLIES SERVED THE PEOPLE OF VANCOUVER'S SKID ROW UNRESERVEDLY FOR 19 YEARS.
"TO GOD BE THE GLORY

Acknowledgments

It was in July of 2020 that I received a 1969 manuscript entitled "Give me Freedom, Jesus". This was a document, submitted to the Salvation Army about the Harbour Light ministry in Vancouver, but was never published. Dr. Fred C. Zarfas was the author. He was a former Salvation Army officer, uperintendent of the Mel Trotter Mission in Grand Rapids, Michigan, a pastor and student of God's Word and was a popular Bible conference speaker. A Zarfas family member discovered the papers in 2002 and they were forwarded to Major Sam Fame at the Harbour Light, where he and his wife were the Executive Directors. Sam has the 'spiritual gift' of hoarding. He is an avid student of history and collects documents wherever he goes. He is also very generous with his findings and much of the research garnered for this book is due to his diligence.

My wife, Joy, several friends and family members, have served as editors and encouragers along the way during this writing. I am so appreciative of their love and support. I contacted Dianne Holland to do a final review. She has been an integral part of Harbour Light and Miracle Valley for many years. Her creativity turned this book into something so much more inspirational than just my research of facts. Something that started out as a Covid- 19 project, to keep me busy, developed into a labor of love and appreciation for an upbringing that few could imagine. Living a life of faith was normal to Bill Leslie, but it was frightening, at times, for those carried along the journey.

These reflections and remembrances will, I hope, encourage you along your life's path. A Facebook group has been formed (**miracle valley/harbour light**). If you want to share your memories, or your family's history, in association with these ministries, your posts and pictures would be most welcome.

Remember - God can do anything!

About the Author

William Paul Leslie has been involved in public ministry for over 40 years. Starting out as a Salvation Army officer in 1972, he served in various appointments for 18 years. In 1973 he and Joy were married and they raised three children. The next opportunity for ministry saw the Leslie's leading the Port Kells Congregational Christian Church (portkellschurch.com) in Surrey, B.C. for nine years. In 2000, Paul was called to be the first Executive Director/Chaplain for the Island Crisis Care Society (iccare.ca) in Nanaimo, B.C. After four years of a growing ministry with I.C.C.S., the Leslie's became involved again in pastoral leadership at the Nanaimo First Baptist Church (fbcnanaimo.ca). Settling in Nanaimo has also allowed them the privilege of seeing their three children married and taking advantage of the opportunities to spoil their five grandchildren.

Paul thought he was retired after a heart attack in 2014, but has

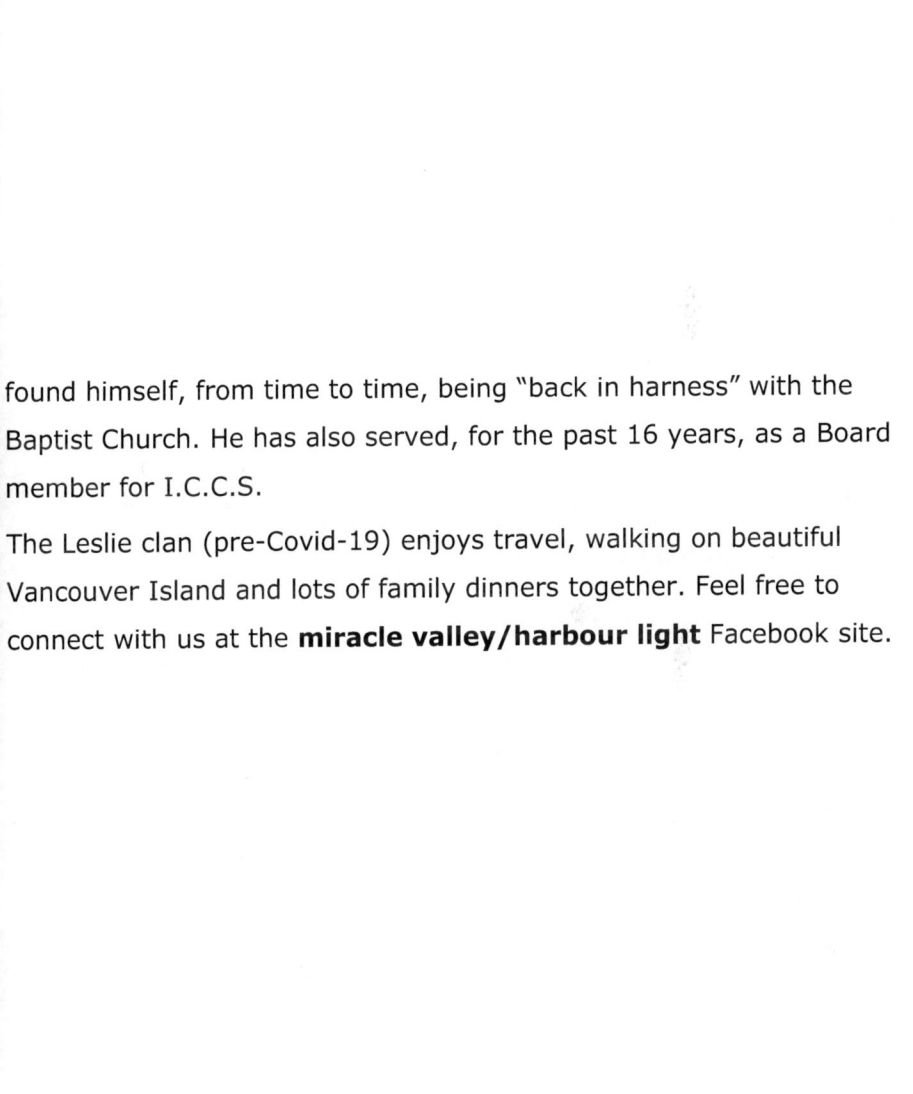

found himself, from time to time, being "back in harness" with the Baptist Church. He has also served, for the past 16 years, as a Board member for I.C.C.S.

The Leslie clan (pre-Covid-19) enjoys travel, walking on beautiful Vancouver Island and lots of family dinners together. Feel free to connect with us at the **miracle valley/harbour light** Facebook site.

Manufactured by Amazon.ca
Bolton, ON